EXECUTIVE TALENT

How to Identify and Develop the Best

Tom Potts

Arnold Sykes

BUSINESS ONE IRWIN
Homewood, Illinois 60430

© RICHARD D. IRWIN, INC., 1993

Sponsoring editor: Cynthia A. Zigmund
Project editor: Gladys True
Production manager: Diane Palmer
Designer: Heidi J. Baughman
Compositor: Impressions, a division of Edwards Brothers, Inc.
Typeface: 11/13 Electra
Printer: Book Press, Inc.

Library of Congress Cataloging-in-Publication Data

Potts, Tom.
    Executive talent : how to identify and develop the best / Tom
Potts, Arnold Sykes.
      p.   cm.
    Includes index.
    ISBN 1-55623-754-5
    1. Career development.   2. Assessment centers (Personnel
management procedure) I. Sykes, Arnold. II. Title.
HF5549.5.C35P68 1993
658.4'07124—dc20   92–16741

Printed in the United States of America

  2 3 4 5 6 7 8 9 0 BP   9 8 7 6 5 4 3

This book is dedicated to our families, who gave us their love, support, and encouragement:

Barbara Potts
Bill and Kim Potts
Nancy and Guy Miller
Martha and Scott Meeks
Linda Sykes
Melissa, Steve, and Mike Sykes

Preface

Thirty years ago I started work in a world-famous multinational company. By way of encouragement, my employers produced an outline of my future career. "This will be your life," they said, "with titles of likely jobs." The outline ended, I remember, with myself as chief executive of a particular company in a particular far-off country. I was, at the time, suitably flattered. I left them long before I reached the heights they planned for me, and by then I knew that not only did the job they had picked out no longer exist, neither did the company I would have directed nor even the country in which I was to have operated.

Charles Handy
The Age of Unreason[1]

Some would say the story above is a perfect example of a succession planning and management development system gone wrong. It might be used by some today as proof that succession planning and management development, that system that has been practiced successfully in many companies for decades, is no longer relevant. Some critics would suggest that the world is simply moving too fast for any organizational planning process that is aimed at directly monitoring and influencing the development of an individual's career. Some might say that managers today are far too independent to either want or tolerate such incursions upon their personal prerogatives and certainly do not welcome any "planned assistance" from the organization to help channel the successful person's career in one direction over another.

Some might say that the worst possible thing to encourage is a system that helps to retain individuals in a single organization over the life of their entire careers—a premise held by many who believe that the only way in which new ideas can be generated or incorporated into an organization's thought processes, debate, or decisions is to purchase fresh thinking from outside the organization. Some might say that it is a poor use of executive time for senior individuals to sit around a table and discuss the performance, progression, successes, and stumbles of individuals one or several levels below those who sit around the table.

Some could say all of the above.

In the pages that follow, we contend that there is great need for the following:

- a system that helps identify the best talent inside the organization and that keeps close touch on performance over time;
- a system that is aimed at optimizing each step in a career progression for people who are the most critical and valued management resources;
- a system that tries to assure the regular and ongoing growth and development of managers within the company so that the organization can retain these valued management resources; and
- a system that is secured and made effective by the full and ongoing commitment of a CEO and other senior executives whose lives (hopefully) have been influenced as a result of time and energy invested in such systems.

It is about such a system and its subparts—fundamental, tried, and proven by many successful organizations—that this book is written. It is about a system that is not only important, but more relevant now than ever before.

We hope it brings value to you.

Tom Potts
Arnold Sykes

Acknowledgments

We genuinely thank those professionals who shared their knowledge with us and allowed us to help convey their ideas to others. These individuals are well recognized both for their contributions to the field of human resources and as strong proponents of management development and succession planning systems. In the order that they were interviewed, they are:

Eric Vetter, Ph.D.,who has been a university professor and executive recruiter and was for many years head of human resources at Gould Inc. and Crocker Bank. Eric was one of the earliest writers on the subject of identifying and developing high potential candidates. His knowledge of succession planning systems, and his even greater contribution to the understanding of concepts of leadership, have had a major impact on our thinking about management development.

Steve McMahon, who was formerly vice president of human resources at Fireman's Fund Insurance, helped us understand the importance of "substance and results" versus "forms and other rituals." Today, as director of human resources at Apple USA, Steve's experience and pragmatism continue to help us gain insight into the importance of developing systems that contribute to the accomplishment of organizations' goals.

Don Laidlaw, who at the time of our interviews was director of Executive Resources at IBM and a board member and later president of the Human Resource Planning Society. Don's willingness to share his and IBM's experience in management development and succession planning has always been very helpful and has continued to have a positive impact on other practitioners.

Walt Trosin was vice president of Human Resources at Merck until early 1992 when he was appointed vice chairman of Fuchs, Cuthrell & Co. of New York. He gave us insight into how management development and succession planning make a genuine contribution to a company that, for years according to *Fortune* surveys, has been one of the most admired corporations in the United States.

We also thank Roger N. Blakeney, Ph.D., director of the Center for Executive Development in the College of Business Administration at the University of Houston, for providing us the opportunity to interact with and be challenged by hundreds of MBA candidates during the past five years. These men and women, mostly corporate professionals and managers, remind us of the tremendous talent, energy, and value inherent in this generation of corporate America. Our thanks go to Bill Maki, director, Human Resources, Weyerhaeuser Company, and president of the Human Resource Planning Society, for information on the review process at Weyerhaeuser and to Dick Holmberg, manager, Compensation & Management Development, Exxon USA, for his review of chapters and constructive comments.

We especially thank Professor James Donnelly of the University of Kentucky for his encouragement and introduction to our publisher and Cynthia Zigmund, senior editor, Business One Irwin, for her guidance through the many months of work.

Seldom is a nonfiction book written about which its writers can say that it came entirely from within. This book is the result of interactions with many individuals through the years. We would like to express our deep appreciation to the many managers and executives in the organizations where we have attempted to ply our trade as management development consultants and succession planning practitioners.

Specifically, Arnold Sykes would like to acknowledge: R. G. Wallace at Phillips Chemical, an early adopter of these concepts and a strong influence on other Phillips executives to follow his lead; Bob Clark, mentor, friend, and my first manager at Phillips, who more than any other person there helped start me down this path of work; Fred Giari, good friend and counselor, who opened the door for me as he made his exit, in an unselfish way I will never forget; Arch Rambeau, vice president of human resources at General Dynamics, who provided the real platform from which to develop and try to sell these concepts internally; Ralph Hawes, head of the Pomona Division of General Dynamics, another early adopter due to the good staff work of Don Carlson; and Norm Silver, director of human resources at Tektronix, who provided the employment opportunity that afforded the greatest challenge up to that time in implementing succession planning. Both Gary Jewkes and I learned the hard lessons that come from trying to sell a solution for which few believed a problem really existed.

The final corporate effort to implement these ideas came at E F Hutton in September 1987. Jay Partin provided both a life boat and another opportunity to work with a large organization. Regrettably, we had barely developed our mutual agenda when, like a puff of smoke on a windy day, E F Hutton no longer existed as an independent company. But those precious months of relative stability, while we watched a company disappear, will never be forgotten. Thanks also to Matt Starcevich, associate at Phillips Petroleum, longtime friend, and founder of the Center for Management & Organization Effectiveness. Matt has always been the person to turn to for calibration. His success with his management coaching tools has reflected his abilities. His guidance over two decades has proven invaluable to me.

Finally we would like to thank our wives, Barbara Potts and Linda Sykes, for their help in preparing chapters, proofreading, providing constructive feedback, and above all for their incredible patience.

T. P.
A. S.

Contents

The Critical Path: Auditing a Mature System, 213
Government and Not-For-Profit Organizations, 215
Why We Are Upbeat About the Future, 217

SECTION

I

MANAGEMENT DEVELOPMENT IN TODAY'S ENVIRONMENT

Chapter One

THE NEW ERA

I dentifying and developing executive talent is not an instantaneous decision or action. It occurs over many years and involves corporate processes usually referred to as management development and succession planning. This is a book about management development and succession planning in changing times. It is about helping employees to achieve their highest potentials, whatever that level may be. ·

But before we can suggest how to, we must address the rapidly changing business and industrial environment that is having considerable impact on the age-old processes of management development.

WHAT HAS CHANGED?

The first lines of *Future Shock*, written in 1970, are: "In the three short decades between now and the twenty-first century, millions of ordinary, psychologically normal people will face an abrupt collision with the future."[1] We are in that third decade, and the future described by Alvin Toffler is now. It is that prophetic change as it applies to the business environment, and the specific need to develop better managers and leaders, that led us to write this book. Other models for succession planning and management development may still be largely applicable. However, during the past decade, enormous and complex changes in business and industry have occurred. The playing field has changed, there are new rules, and the tried and proven strategies are no longer guaranteed to produce winning results.

These changes are having an extraordinary impact on the lives of employees. Organizations that were considered sacred in terms of stability and security have been severely altered, if not eliminated, along with thousands of executive and managerial positions. We now realize that no organization, regardless of size or strength, is immune from being acquired or from having substantial parts of itself sold off.

International business is no longer just the domain of super corporations. Even relatively modest enterprises are opening plants overseas and searching out new markets. As a growing segment of American industry continues to move into worldwide markets, management and management development will take on an international flavor. The importing of foreign-born managers into U.S. operations will add cultural diversity to the executive suites. More Americans will be working for foreign employers, and some will be asked to take up permanent residency in foreign countries to further their careers. But because of the difficulty of moving families internationally, more executives will move to other companies rather than leave these shores.

Executives are moving to new positions in unprecedented numbers. Generally employees are perceived to be less loyal and less willing to make personal sacrifices for the furtherance of their careers. In a survey of human resource executives, we asked for their estimate of the change in employee loyalty between 1980 and 1991. It was no surprise that over two-thirds of the respondents reported a decrease in company loyalty by professional and technical employees and that more than half reported a decrease in loyalty by managers and executives. (The complete survey is in the Appendix.)

In the eyes of financial institutions and shareholders, corporate worth has become so volatile that management tends to place a higher priority on short-term performance than on long-term organizational viability. To many executives, long-range human resources planning seems less relevant today.

The intense pressures to reduce costs have introduced a new set of buzz words—"delayering," "downsizing," and "rightsizing"—that tend to describe organizations with fewer management positions and that are more responsive, efficient, and productive. For the most part, we see these moves toward greater organizational efficiency as being very positive. But they do have considerable influence on the historical process of identifying and developing executive talent. Fewer positions are available for advancement and they come open less frequently.

Corporate decision making is now a public matter. In many states, "sunshine laws" were enacted to prevent closed-door decisions by legislatures and government officials. But today, the media have invaded the corporate executive offices as well. When the staff of "60 Minutes" places a call to an executive suite today, it will be a rare executive who first thinks, "This may be an opportunity for us to publicize our good work." The more likely reaction is, "Why us?"

The suggestion that executive decision making is now in the public domain is not intended to imply that it is wrong. Rather, it says that executives, in making decisions on succession and in establishing policies on all aspects of human resources management, must contend with the public's reaction as well as the business benefits and risks of the decision.

For better or worse, the public perceives corporate integrity as being low. Bad news always gets more publicity and bigger headlines than good news. Never mind that countless corporations are impeccably honest, strive to be fair to customers and employees, and make a genuine contribution to the community. The public perception is that corporations today are less stable and secure. Ten or 20 years ago, society tended to frown on giving up a good job and career for other employment. The public now perceives that no corporation offers a guarantee of secure employment, and the recent record of abrupt terminations would support that view. Parents who in the past might have counseled their adult children against leaving an employer are now more likely to say, "Go for it!"

It has become old-fashioned to think of corporate loyalty as a virtue. There is enough evidence of the hurt caused by loyal employees whose jobs have been eliminated. It is not only the employees themselves who are less loyal. It is society that believes that employees should not feel any particular loyalty. Moreover, in some cases, loyalty has given way to hostility. This shift became most apparent when we met with an Executive MBA class to discuss management development. These students were middle managers whose tuition was paid by their employers and who attended class partly on company time. To our surprise, some expressed open hostility toward their senior management and little faith in the working of the management development systems within their particular companies. Some indicated that even as they attended the program, they were looking outside for better opportunities. No one stood up to defend his or her company or management.

EMPLOYEE LOYALTY

The change in employee loyalty is the most talked about and probably the most significant of the changes in the environment of management development. We offer these candid opinions.

Employees (including managers) have witnessed much in the past decade that has completely destroyed or severely damaged their confidence in the corporation and its leadership. They have seen senior management do everything to take care of itself with little or no apparent concern for those at levels below. They have seen many executives in corporate America sacrifice virtually everything on the altar of short-term profitability. They have seen leaders tolerate incompetence, yet extol the organization to perform better, quicker, and more productively. They have seen senior executives almost powerless to prevent unwanted advances upon the organization by external forces. And they have seen the disruption to the organization created by the hastily conceived defenses against hostile takeovers. They have seen their peers and, for the younger employees, fathers and mothers who, after giving the best years of their lives, are tossed aside or early-retired in a corporate restructuring.

Many employees and managers at the midcareer stage have concluded that indeed the organization does not have a heart nor much of a memory. Since the company has not been loyal to the individual, they reason that it would be naive or short-sighted to show loyalty to the corporation.

Over the past decade many thousands, perhaps hundreds of thousands, of employees have seen the dreadful results from exceedingly poor, inept, and uncaring behavior on the part of corporate leadership. They have said to themselves, "Is this whom I am supposed to look up to? Is this who is really steering the ship? Is this who is looking out for my security and long-term interests?"

These strong words are not intended to indict all corporate management. On the contrary, the vast majority of corporate executives today are caring, decent, and honest. Yet these harsh words do reflect the prevailing atmosphere of employees' distrust of internal management development.

Throughout this book, we will address the most significant implications for management development that arise from the loss of employee loyalty. First, employee expectations are more focused on short-term rewards than on long-term opportunity because they doubt that long-term opportunity even exists. Second, even where a management development system is operating, employees have little confidence in it. Third, confidence in the management development system is undermined by recruiting executives from the outside. Finally, with few advancement opportunities, new ways are needed to motivate professionals and managers to a high level of performance.

EMPLOYEE VALUES

A senior executive for a multinational corporation commented that he had moved his family 19 times in the course of his company career. Today, that would be viewed as ridiculous. No corporation should expect or demand so much personal sacrifice. Contrast that with a professional or manager who spends many months away from home helping manage an environmental disaster. Because of the unusual demands placed on a corporation by that kind of emergency, such a sacrifice is reasonable. The point of these two examples is that employee values are not stand-alone positions. They are greatly influenced by corporate need and the contribution to be made. And they are influenced by the needs of the employee and the employee's family. An employee may willingly give up a series of weekends to work on a company project that is important and for which his or her participation is vital. However, that same employee may not be willing to make the commitment if the project is perceived as nonessential and for which his or her contribution is marginal. Values have not changed, but the perception of the need for contribution has.

Much has been written about the baby boomers, many of whom are now in their thirties and forties and are part of middle management. These are the people, similar to those in the Executive MBA class, who have lost confidence in the ability of their employers to provide for their careers. There is another group that has arrived on the corporate scene, the "baby busters." One observer makes the case that the baby busters, after two or three years with a corporation, see the personal sacrifices being made by the boomers and decide it is not for them.[2] A number of busters indicate they will not commit to the long hours and pressures perceived as necessary to get ahead. Although this could mean that the values of the younger set have changed because they are more attuned to family and personal fulfillment than to material wealth and getting ahead, the interpretation may not be quite that simple. Many new employees correctly perceive that there are fewer opportunities ahead for them. Therefore, they do not aspire to positions that they are unlikely to achieve. In addition, employees in dual-income families may have lower career aspirations because of lower financial needs.

There has always been a segment of the professional and managerial workforce that makes a conscious choice to forgo advancement for a preferred life-style. Conversely, there has always been a segment that makes great sacrifices for advancement opportunity. We believe that there is still an ample workforce of qualified professionals and managers who will sacrifice to attain advancement.

The change in employee values, then, may not be the issue. Some employees will make personal sacrifices and some won't. What has changed is that employees are less willing to make personal sacrifice where they do not see the corporate need and where they do not feel they are making a worthy contribution. Still, there are some basic things corporations can do to earn the loyalty and trust of their employees:

1. Create an environment in which both employees and managers are given meaningful, challenging, and interesting work.
2. Create an environment in which everyone's efforts are recognized and rewarded.
3. Create an environment in which individuals are regularly kept informed, ideas are sought out, and employees are listened to.
4. Create an environment in which there is a presence of effective manager and leader role models.

DOWNSIZING AND CORPORATE SURVIVAL

Downsizing was inevitable. Corporations in every conceivable business became fat during successful years of growth and diversification. But once the "D" movement started, everyone had to jump on the bandwagon to stay alive. In *Downsizing: Reshaping the Corporation for the Future*, Robert Tomasko makes the interesting observation that in 1980 managers made up about 10 percent of the U.S. industrial workforce as compared with 4 percent in Japan and 3 percent in Germany.[3] It's no wonder so many U.S. "reduction in force" programs have targeted managers! We were ripe for downsizing.

Of course, the implication for management development is that fewer management positions are available for the reasonable advancement of candidates with executive potential. Downsizing or "rightsizing" as it is now more appropriately called, is irreversible. While the wave of mergers, acquisitions, spin-offs, and other financially driven reorganizations is rapidly subsiding, the layers and management positions eliminated by rightsizing are not likely to ever be reinstated. Overall, rightsizing is healthy for business, and we believe it offers some opportunities and challenges for management development.

First of all, the reduced number of management and staff jobs available is a mixed blessing. Planning and implementing career development moves becomes more of a challenge. Yet remaining jobs are likely to present more meaningful opportunities for growth. But with each position having to carry its own weight, it becomes more difficult and riskier to move inexperienced people into jobs for which there are no longer other people to "carry the candidate." Again, there is a positive side to this. People grow faster in these situations, and a more accurate assessment of their potential can be made, even though there is less room for error. Another challenge is that in a lean organization, it is difficult to pull people out for training, task forces, and other assignments that have previously been useful in development and in assessing potential. Good people will plateau earlier, requiring innovation in order to motivate them without availability of the "carrot" of continuous promotion.

Finally, downsized organizations have experienced a tremendous exodus of experience. This loss of knowledge cannot be replaced overnight. Many companies are calling back retirees on a contract basis to help, which is a good solution. But until the experience level is built back over time, there is an added risk in decision making and in operations. The good news on this particular aspect of downsizing is that in some instances, an organization learns that the "vital contribution" it thought it was receiving from an individual in reality is not that great a loss.

There is no question that a lean, no-nonsense environment is better for individual growth than is one that is stodgy and bureaucratic. Overall, the results in downsizing in corporate America are positive. However, downsizing greatly challenges the process of internal management development.

Corporate survival is now an issue. In recent years, the month of December has become "brag time" for investment banking. Typically, a two-page advertisement in *The Wall Street Journal* will list all of the mergers, sales, and acquisitions that a prestigious investment banking house has brought about during the year. For example, the 1990 year-end ad for Lehman Brothers listed more than 150 transactions, eight in excess of $1 billion each.[4] (The top listing was for a "successful defense," which sounds like use of the really big guns!) Of course, each transaction has a different story, and many transactions may be good for the survival of both corporations. But some of the reported successes will likely mean the demise of corporations of long standing.

Unfortunately, what we learn about some recent mergers would indicate that little consideration is given to the human resources. In the bestseller,

Barbarians at the Gate: The Fall of RJR Nabisco, Burrough and Helyar record an exciting account of one of America's largest corporate takeovers.[5] They paint a picture of anxious analysts, working late into the night, poring over financial records to determine the true value of a corporation. However, there is no indication that consideration was ever given to the value of the company's human assets.

Traditional management development systems were based on the assumption that the corporation, and its need for executives, was forever. Today that would be a bad assumption. As we will discuss later, management development works best when executives and managers can devote their energies to the development of others. When executives become consumed over their own plights and the development of their own golden parachutes, they have little incentive for devoting time to the management development of others. Employees quickly sense the disinterest of their senior executives, and they in turn lose confidence in the system for internal growth and development. Good people will have their résumés out on the street.

There is no easy answer to the corporate survival issue. Few corporations are totally immune to merger or acquisition. And it is clear that many modern day chief executives are prone to make decisions based on financial return with little regard for the survival of the corporate entity. Business schools are not teaching executives to be responsible for the preservation of the business.

It would be naive to suggest that corporations should not be subject to externally generated change. Still, the threat of that change plays havoc with the desire to develop management talent in an orderly fashion. For better or worse, the perception as well as the fact of corporate survival has changed, which has serious implications for the development of executives. However, a cloud on corporate survival is not sufficient reason to abandon, delay, or de-emphasize the practice of management development. It makes the process more challenging, but the challenge can and should be met.

CHAPTER CHECK LIST

The lexicon of management science contains such expressions as "managing change" and "change agent" as if change is something you wrap your arms around and use to make good things happen. Unfortunately, some of the changes identified in this chapter do not readily lend themselves to use for the betterment of management development. Yet there are some positive changes:

1. Decisions involving people will be weighed against a higher standard of corporate integrity. The decisions must be right for all parties, including employees. The need for employee sacrifices, including relocations, must be clear and easily understood. Employees will be treated with complete candor and respect.

2. Corporate management must now earn employee loyalty and respect. Loyalty will no longer be blindly given.

3. Jobs will be more challenging and personally rewarding, will have more substance, and will require visible contribution. The throw-away jobs used in the past for management development no longer exist. Individuals will grow more rapidly, and they can be better tested.

4. An ethnically and gender-diverse workforce will be seen by enlightened management more for its benefits than for its obligations.

And there are challenges to:

5. Demonstrate that management development systems are still viable and that they should not be totally abandoned (as has happened in so many firms today).

6. Develop a practical approach to management development that will allow the system to function in a highly changing business environment.

Chapter Two

INTERNAL MANAGEMENT DEVELOPMENT

T o us, the most persuasive argument for an internal management development system is that the growth of executive talent takes long years with a variety of experiences and training. Graduates from advanced academic programs are not likely to have the talent or wisdom to take over as chief executives without years of growth and experience. If all corporations assume that good talent can be hired away from other companies, who then is going to develop that talent? Using the analogy of professional baseball, if each major league team got rid of its farm system because it thought that enough good players could be hired away from other teams, what would develop the players?

There will always be a number of companies with management development systems, and companies without their own systems can still recruit executive candidates from other companies. For example, General Electric, along with many other corporations, is likely to remain a provider of executive talent. A recent edition of *Fortune* listed nine CEOs who had formerly been officers, mostly vice presidents and higher, at General Electric. The *Fortune* column was appropriately headed "General Electric as CEO Boot Camp."[1]

Executives can also gain experience by having multicompany careers. But counting on other companies to develop executives can be a hit or miss approach when compared to the development that can be planned within one organization.

Our bottom line is that good executives don't grow on trees. They are "grown" by responsible corporations that provide, over a period of many years, the nurturing and developmental experiences necessary to equip individuals to master the ultimate executive responsibilities. It is therefore essential that each corporation have a system to grow its own executives. We will discuss some of the reasons often put forth for not having an internal system for the development of managers and executives. And we will give some of our reasons for believing that such a system is important to any corporation.

CHANGE REQUIRES MORE PLANNING

As discussed in chapter 1, the business environment is changing faster than ever before. Rapid change is easier to cope with when responses are anticipated from within than when external events are allowed to control the actions. Because plans may become quickly out-of-date, they must be continually monitored and adjusted. Planning today is difficult, compared to that required in a more stable environment, but that does not make it less essential. There are several reasons we believe that succession planning and management development are more important today than ever before.

Having a management development plan helps attract good candidates for employment. A question we are often asked by students who are considering a new employment or career change is, "How can I determine whether a prospective employer really practices management development and will provide internal career growth opportunity?" Our polling of students indicates that virtually all of them would prefer to work for companies that provide internal management development.

It is true that today, many employment candidates do not expect that they will complete a career with one corporation, and we do not suggest that the presence of a management development system will be what primarily attracts a candidate for employment. But they would prefer employment with companies in which the opportunity for growth in one organization is present. As always, the very best students will have several employment options and will be more discerning about the management development practices of prospective employers, even though the quest for job satisfaction and the ability to contribute will be much higher on the list of things looked for by a quality candidate.

Savvy magazine publishes an annual list of companies at which growth opportunities for women appear to be greatest. The companies on the list are known for their training and development programs. They monitor the progress of young employees, provide responsibilities early, and accelerate development opportunities. It is commendable to be such an employer and to be so recognized. Whether these companies can retain highly qualified and sought-after female (and male) employees depends on the experiences gained and the opportunities perceived while the employee is on the job.

The freedom with which executives move among corporations today means that succession plans must now include a greater depth of replacements in anticipation of higher attrition. More candidates need to be included in succession plans and individual development plans must be improved. Development plans need to reflect the individual's input regarding personal goals, as well as management's views about the individual's future. Moreover, it takes far more planning to provide for orderly growth and for succession in an environment in which leading high-potential candidates may be lost without notice. Key to the planning process is flexibility and bench strength to meet such contingencies.

Having two careers—the employee's and the employee's spouse—to consider has added a dimension to corporate planning for management development. A corporation's ability to relocate its employee may be limited by the possibility that the spouse's job and career will take precedence in the family, thereby negating management development plans for the company's employee.

Another reason that succession planning is important is that employees expect more information. The employer must plan with more precision and with a higher degree of involvement from the employee.

There will be fewer management openings, also suggesting the need for more planning. As early as 1987, Robert M. Tomasko, a writer and consultant specializing in organization planning, suggested that between 1,000 to 2,500 management jobs per company had been lost in many Fortune 500 businesses.[2] The attack on middle management positions has continued as many of the blue chip firms pare down. Companies such as Shell, Exxon, Chevron, General Motors, IBM, Xerox, Westinghouse, and a host of other household names would be included on a current list. In fact, it is highly unlikely that any major corporation has *not* reduced the number of management jobs during the past several years. This compares with the 1970s, when many of these same firms were growing and management ranks were swelling. With fewer management opportunities, firms today have less room for error in staffing decisions. Each position vacancy involves a unique development opportunity that may not be repeated; therefore, the planning behind each move must reflect more thought. In the downsized organization, each position must carry full responsibility; thus, the planning to fill that position becomes even more critical.

There is an urgent need for management diversity. As we will discuss in chapter 8, there is a business need as well as a moral need to increase the participation of minorities and women in management. The fact that efforts to date have been so dismal would highlight the need for more and better planning to recruit, retain, and promote these employees.

Finally, as we pointed out earlier, employee loyalty to the organization is not what it used to be. Given the track record of many organizations, employees are less inclined to hold their employer in high regard and more inclined to look out for themselves first. This loss of loyalty probably has greatest impact in the middle management ranks because the attitudes of middle managers affect the vast number of employees at lower levels.

Hay Research surveyed 750,000 middle managers on how they rated their companies in the period 1988–1990. Only 55 percent expressed a favorable attitude on whether the companies were good places to work, a decline from the 65 percent of those surveyed in the 1985–1987 period. A favorable attitude regarding the ability of top management also declined, from 54 percent to 38 percent.[3] In our survey of human resource executives (see the Appendix), we asked them to measure loyalty (on a scale of 1 to 10, 10 being best) of professional employees and managers for 1980 and 1991. The responses indicated their perception that loyalty had significantly decreased over the decade:

	1980	1991
Professional Employees	7.6	5.5
Managers and Executives	8.2	6.8

The loss of employee loyalty challenges the corporation to be credible in its handling of placements and promotions. Senior management must attend to the development of each employee and to the planning of careers toward the individual's highest potential. Even then, there is no guarantee that employees will not leave. But with the increased level of planning in areas of management development, fewer good employees will be enticed to defect.

PROVIDING A GOOD WORKPLACE

Good workplaces assume that a firm's growth is due largely to the efforts of the people working there. So they have policies and practices that offer those people the opportunity to grow with the enterprise. For this reason, promotion from within is gospel at virtually all good workplaces.

Robert Levering, A Great Place to Work.[4]

Based on Levering's research, it follows that one of the practices chief executives would want to put in place is a system for internal development. Of course, there is more logic to providing a good workplace than just altruism or a desire to be among the leaders. A good workplace attracts, retains, and motivates quality employees. Young professionals and managers with whom we talked have expressed an almost unanimous view that "opportunity" is an important quality in their assessment of potential employers, supporting Levering's view that providing a good workplace and providing for internal development go hand in hand.

Levering gives another reason to encourage a policy of promotion from within: uncovering hidden talent. He uses the example of Delta Air Lines. When Delta needed two staff writers for the company newspaper, the newspaper's editor believed it would be necessary to hire them from the outside. But as part of Delta's "promote from within" policy, the job was posted. Nearly 100 employees responded, eighteen with journalism degrees. As Levering reports, "such a policy lets employees feel that they are considered capable of growth and that they are recognized as more than a ticket agent, a stewardess, or whatever job slot they happen to occupy."[5] Although this example is not about *executive* development, the benefits that come from employees feeling that they are considered capable of growth applies to people at all levels of an organization.

ENTREPRENEURSHIP

People who do not support the principles of internal management development usually point out that such a system discourages the entrepreneurship that has played such a part in the success of many corporations. T. Boone Pickens, Jr., described his feelings in his autobiography:

I got a close look at the men who had made it to the top of some big companies. They had a lot in common; most of them had spent their entire working lives in one organization. I could see at first hand why the entrepreneurs in those companies had become frustrated and gone on to something else. . . . After getting to know the Good Ol' Boys, I realized only a few had ever made any money on their own. . . . They were bureaucrats, caretakers. They had learned to move up through the bureaucracy with a minimum of personal risk. It was a special talent, and not one I wanted. By the time they reached the top, they weren't interested in opinions other than their own. They were out of touch with reality.[6]

Those of us who have been around big corporations sense some validity in Boone Pickens's comments, which might suggest some questions about a system for internal management development:

1. Do such systems breed mediocrity?
2. Do executives become the clones of existing management?
3. Is individuality lost?
4. Is entrepreneurship stifled?
5. Is risk taking discouraged?

The questions have some basis, but not, in our view, as an indictment of internal management development. Rather they should be taken as cautions to be addressed by those implementing a management development system.

Pickens mentions Exxon as one of the Good Ol' Boy companies and uses the example of Exxon's purchase of Reliance Electric Company as "one of the worst deals in the history of corporate America."[7] Even if true, one bad deal does not necessarily reflect a lack of entrepreneurship or an unwillingness to take risk. Actually, these are characteristics that are highly valued in assessing potential in many corporations today. So we strongly disagree with the implications of Pickens's statement, although we do believe he has identified problems that can occur in any organization, regardless of whether executives are developed from within or hired from outside.

INTERNAL COMPETITION AND TEAM EFFECTIVENESS

W. Edwards Deming, whose "prescription for quality" has been embraced by hundreds, perhaps even thousands, of companies, makes the case that competition within an organization is counterproductive. Deming says:

"We are all born with intrinsic motivation, self-esteem, dignity, an eagerness to learn. Our present system of management crushes that all out. . . . Of course [competition] is bad. People then work for the grade. In school, they studied for the grade; not to learn anything, but for the grade."[8]

If we understand Deming's philosophy, it is that having people continually concerned for their own appraisal and ranking takes away from their contribution toward the team results. To use a sports analogy, a player should be concerned only with the team's winning, not with his or her performance statistics.

But is that the real world? Competition is a part of our lives whether we like it or not. We agree with the common belief that organizations do best when they do not pit individual members against one another. However, this does not mean that organizations can remove all vestiges of competition from the way they operate. We believe that enlightened management can and does do much to promote team effort without totally eliminating internal competition. In fact, a major quality considered in the competition for promotion will be the employee's ability to be a team player.

By its very nature, management development involves many individuals growing over time, orchestrated by an internal management development process toward an ever-decreasing number of more important positions. It is the very essence of competition, and it is unrealistic in today's environment to believe that employees will not feel that they are competing with their peers for recognition and advancement.

The challenge in management development is to use competition positively, fairly, and productively. Good employees will view competition positively, but only if they feel that promotions are fairly determined. And without a rational, well-run management development system, it is unlikely that fairness can be achieved.

COMBATTING RELUCTANCE

Seldom do senior executives publicly state that they believe a system for internal management development is wrong. At the very least, they will admit that there is some advantage in having succession planning. Yet they will rationalize why a system for management development and succession planning is not right for their organization! We offer some of the comments we have heard along with our responses:

We have just been through downsizing and more is to follow. To have a system of management development when few management opportunities will exist would be misleading to the employees.

Our response is to point out that the need for good managers is greatest in tough economic times. Failure to provide a system that identifies management talent and seeks out ways to maximize or leverage personal growth opportunities, and also accomplishes work, will cause better employees to leave, compounding the problems of downsizing.

Over the past decade, researchers for the nonprofit Center for Creative Leadership in Greensboro, North Carolina, have asked hundreds of senior executives: "What essentially provided the greatest boost to your learning process? What caused you to grow and develop? What more than anything is responsible for the success that you enjoy today?" Many respondents said that "being provided with tough assignments, being put into demanding jobs (something I didn't think I was ready for) or being put into project situations under demanding conditions with exacting deadlines."[9]

Downsizing provides opportunities for managerial and executive growth that should be exploited through the careful planning for management development.

Moreover, with fewer opportunities for promotion and movement, attention must be given to development through the job itself. According to the Center for Creative Leadership, corporations need to realize the potential that exists for developing executives simply through their assigned responsibilities.

We have found that the forecasts of future management needs in a downsized organization are usually underestimated. There will still be normal attrition, but of greater concern is the attrition by employees who will voluntarily seek opportunities on the outside.

Finally, we would suggest that the employees be asked whether or not they would consider the presence of a management development system as misleading. The results might be surprising.

Our company is on the block for merger or acquisition.

Good executives will be concerned about how their employees will fare after the change. The greatest service that can be provided is to have a system that identifies the talents and experiences of each individual employee. Otherwise, talents will not be utilized and employees may be shortchanged. How regrettable, if after a merger, the new corporation goes outside to hire individuals for positions for which current employees are genuinely qualified. An employee who has spent several years with one of the merged firms could feel that his or her contribution has been totally wasted. It would, in effect, mean starting over.

For the new firm to hit the ground running, it is important that qualified and experienced people fill key positions. With the likelihood that many employees will be surplus, a management development system will be needed to identify both the talent and experience required for each new position and those individuals who are most qualified. Employees who lack the necessary qualifications should be the primary candidates for retraining for work in a new area or, in the worst case, terminated. Realistically, it is hard to conceive of a merger where the balance sheet of executive resources is not a critical part of the decision. Yet according to informal surveys we have taken, very often the human assets are not given significant consideration by the merger team.

We have put so much responsibility on our managers already that they just don't have time to work on management development and succession planning. It would be nice to do, but we just can't afford it with our limited staffing.

The issue of having the right individual for the right job at the right time becomes one of costs and priorities. It is as simple as "where" the organization wishes to incur the expense. Business executives might be amazed at the time, effort, and expense incurred by firms like Maryland Bank, N.A., the credit card bank, when it interviews candidates for employment. But results speak for themselves. According to chair and CEO Charles Cawley, the employee turnover rate at MBNA is 25 percent of that of companies in its market.[10]

We believe it costs more *not* to operate a system for internal development. Executive searches are not inexpensive. In addition to out-of-pocket cost are the far greater yet intangible costs of the position remaining vacant while a search is being conducted, plus the lag time required for a new person from outside the organization to get up to speed and oriented to the new culture. (We might add that the employees called on to fill in while the position is vacant, who then train and carry the new manager while he or she learns the company and the job, may not display the highest morale!)

The issue of priorities really is, "What is the value of executive resources to the future of the corporation?" If the value is high, as we believe it should be, then management development should be given the highest priority.

I know my employees. The succession plan is in my head and I don't want my managers or human resources staff getting involved.

This response most likely comes from a CEO who has personally brought his or her firm from a modest beginning to a substantial success. Personal judgments about people have produced good results, and it is difficult for the CEO to involve others in that responsibility. Yet a CEO's lifetime is finite, and it seems obvious that an orderly planning for the development of the future managers should be consistent with the CEO's desire to leave the company in good hands.

In one large firm, the CEO would not entertain the idea of having a formal system for succession planning, believing that the system "was in his head." Yet when time came for his retirement, there was no replacement. He brought in an executive from a different business, who did not work out, and the former CEO came back to run the company. In the meantime, several key executives had left. The core problem remained unresolved.

We are too small to need an internal management development system.

We are frequently asked how large an organization should be before it needs succession planning and management development. We believe the need exists, to some degree, in virtually all organizations. Depending on the nature of the business, a small company of one or two hundred employees could have as many as a dozen key positions and an even greater number of professionals and managers who are candidates to fill those positions. The management development system need not be complex or elaborate. But it should address potential, training, development, career-pathing, and succession planning as does a corporate plan for tens of thousands of employees.

We also believe that employees in smaller firms deserve the same opportunities for growth, development, and internal promotion as do those in large corporations. A management development system is the means of addressing that obligation. Executives of small firms who have trouble accepting our opinion might want to ask their employees how they would feel about a system for management development.

We are too busy growing.

We heard this statement from an executive in a high-tech growth firm. No doubt, it was meant to convey that the time for succession planning would come after the period of rapid growth. But unfortunately, the lead time required to "grow" the executives to manage the larger, more stable corporation foreseen is great. Waiting until things settle down (if they ever do) may be too late. Again, we would suggest asking the employees what they think.

A BASEBALL ANALOGY

George F. Will, writer, columnist, and TV commentator, is also a baseball fan. In the Introduction to *Men at Work: The Craft of Baseball*, Will wrote: "Baseball is as much a mental contest as a physical one. The pace of the action is relentless: There is barely enough time between pitches for all the thinking that is required, and that the best players do, in processing the changing information about the crucial variables."[11] Substitute the word "business" for "baseball," "decisions" for "pitches," and "managers" for "players," and the statement would be pertinent to business today. Thus, at least for baseball fans, George Will gives a lead-in for extending an analogy to employee development.

Professional baseball has always demonstrated the value of succession planning and player development. The succession planning process for each position on a major league team rivals the process used by any large corporation for its key positions. Baseball executives, managers, and coaches spend countless hours reviewing and discussing player performance and potential. No player is overlooked, and for each position at each level there is a list of backup candidates. The job of the coach is to counsel and instruct to help players overcome their shortcomings.

Baseball uses a farm system of minor league teams to identify, train, and develop its future stars. The developmental process is internal and vertical. Young players usually are assigned to minor league teams to begin their development and advancement until they reach the majors. In recent years, the number of minor leagues has declined, so that players move through fewer levels to the top. In fact, baseball may have been one of the first industries to recognize the need for leaner, flatter organizations.

Now that there are fewer minor league teams available for player development, there is less time for skill development, and many players start nearer the top. The farm system is producing fewer talented players, and even mediocre performers demand enormous salaries. Players no longer remain forever the property of one organization. They can become free agents and they hire agents themselves to negotiate their contracts. As free agents, their loyalty is to their own careers. It may be well into the season before fans begin to associate star players with their new teams.

Player attitudes have also changed. A generation ago, a ball player would play out each season in the minors, perhaps for 10 years, always hoping that someday his talent would blossom and he would be on his way to big-league stardom. Most players never made it. Even today, you may meet some old-timer who will reminisce about his professional baseball days with the Cardinals (or some other) organization. The word "organization"—spoken ever so softly—would mean that he was signed by the St. Louis Cardinals, but never made it to the majors.

Like baseball, business has in the past depended on a kind of farm system. And like the system of baseball leagues, the modern business organization has been downsized so that there are now fewer levels and positions. Like baseball players, business managers and professionals today are less patient with slow career progress. They want to move up quickly and have less loyalty to the corporation and more to their own careers. Potential corporate executives who appear on succession planning documents in most companies did not generally get there because of any tendencies toward relaxation or because they showed great patience with their personal career growth. They are the achievers of the organization who are rarely content to stay in one role of responsibility for very long.

Traditionally, neither baseball players nor business professionals had much say in determining the course of their own careers. Decisions on training, development, and job assignment were made by others. This paternalism has become old-fashioned and is out of step with employees' wishes to have a say, a choice, in decisions affecting their lives. Of course, we see this as progress. In baseball, where players were indentured to one owner or employer for their playing careers, this recognition of an individual's rights is a very positive change. In business, there may not have been the same tight control or ownership of the individual, but the feeling that the employee was trapped by a one-company career was quite real.

Before concluding that baseball should serve as the model for career development, we will point out some differences.

Individual performance statistics are accurate measurements of capabilities for baseball players. Batting averages, runs batted in, home runs, stolen bases, earned run averages—all can accurately measure the performance and promotability of a player. In business, it is not so easy to measure the performance of an individual manager or executive. Corporate or unit performance can be measured and can be very useful. But the direct relationship between the individual executive's performance and the corporation's performance can be fuzzy (if not downright misleading), unrelated, or tangential. In many cases, actual corporate achievements in financial performance are more likely to come from the vision, strategic direction, and investments of past CEOs, rather than from the CEO who may be currently receiving the credit.

While baseball players can become immediately effective when changing teams, a business professional might not be so fortunate when taking on new responsibilities or making a lateral move to another corporation. Sure, the player must learn new signals from the coaches, but his ability to bat, field, or throw does not involve his teammates. On the other hand, the business executive depends heavily on other team members, regardless of his or her individual management skills. A baseball player is primarily an individual performer; an effective executive is just the opposite.

Baseball players are not held back when opportunity beckons. If the Houston Astros need a player immediately from the Tucson farm club, the Astros do not think about how the loss of that player will affect the Tucson team. The player will pack his bag and head for the major league stadium to join his new teammates. This is not always true in business, where there is a natural tendency in an operating division or subsidiary to deny or delay opportunity to an individual who is greatly needed where he or she is. "Not now, maybe in six months," or "We just don't think that is the right job." Delay, stalling, or an outright no is unfortunately an all too typical business response.

Nonetheless, there are lessons that we can draw from baseball:

1. Baseball has demonstrated that a move from a closed, paternalistic system to one that recognizes individual rights and solicits input does not obviate the need for concerted developmental efforts.

2. A corporate "farm system" should feed key executive positions just as it does in major league baseball. Obviously, the system is far more complex in business. But there are lower levels of the corporate organization from which to access talent, and there are logical steps of progression.

3. Any developmental system must be built on the concept of freedom of choice and the understanding that key employees will be attracted to move elsewhere if better opportunities exist. This should prompt management to expend more energy in seeing that employees are recognized and that their jobs are challenging and fulfilling. Management's responsibility is to construct jobs in such a way that employees want to stay and be a part of the current team.

4. Advancement opportunities should not be denied because an employee is too valuable in his or her own assignment or organization. Managers should take pride in seeing employees from their own divisions or organizations succeed and look upon vacancies as opportunities for less senior employees. Management encourages this

behavior when it extends formal recognition and tangible rewards to managers and executives who regularly grow other managers. Individual executives in corporations will tend to be either net exporters or net receivers of other management talent, depending upon what the corporate culture rewards and recognizes as the desired behavior. Most executives recognize that the CEO is the primary "value setter" of that culture.

5. Just as baseball management expends great energy in evaluating player performance and potential, business executives should expend energy in evaluating their employees, particularly those who show high potential.

6. Developmental needs should be identified and met with new experiences, coaching, and training. Baseball does this well. In *Men at Work*, George Will recognizes the teaching skills of the late batting instructor Charlie Lau, who has probably gained more fame as a coach than as a player. Will refers to George Brett of the Kansas City Royals as "the most famous work of art" of batting instructor Lau—a real tribute to a teacher![12]

7. Since business does not have the clear measures of performance and capabilities for executives as does baseball for its players, efforts to develop better measures of executive performance and capability should be a high priority. The slow evolution toward competency-based assessments and more rational approaches to defining job requirements are positive steps.

CHAPTER CHECK LIST

1. Executive talent is the product of years of personal development gained through a variety of work experiences. It does not happen overnight, and it should not be left to some other company to develop. Good executives don't grow on trees!

2. The drastic changes in organization structure brought about by downsizing, mergers, and acquisitions call for *more* planning for the development of executive resources, not less. The fewer management positions available must be efficiently used in the developmental process.

3. Employees are less loyal to their companies and are more likely to seek career opportunities elsewhere. Viable management develop-

ment systems will give good employees more incentive to continue to pursue their careers with their present employer.

4. Providing a good workplace, certainly the objective of any responsible employer, includes providing a system for internal development and growth.

5. Concerns over loss of entrepreneurship or adverse impact of competition can be addressed in the design of a management development system. The negative aspects are usually more than offset by the benefits of orderly management development.

6. If priorities are properly ordered, senior management will always make time available to support and operate a management development system.

7. The move from a closed, paternalistic organization to one that places emphasis on individual rights increases the need for an internal management development system.

Chapter Three

INTEGRATION WITH STRATEGIC BUSINESS PLANNING

G iven the difficulty organizations have in determining the specific direction for their businesses, it is no surprise that they face a greater challenge in synchronizing their succession and management development plans with their overall strategic planning. In its simplest terms, the integration of "people planning" with business planning means assuring that when the strategic decisions are being made regarding direction of the business, thought is being given to the development of key executives and managers, and vice versa. Later we will discuss this integration in terms of what we call "the four P's"—*people, processes, positions*, and *programs.*

CONDITIONS FOR SUCCESSFUL INTEGRATION

Four conditions are needed for successful integration:

1. A clearly defined statement of the mission and business purpose for the organization
2. A supportive corporate culture
3. A perception that management development and succession planning are strategic priorities
4. Credibility in the human resources (HR) organization

Clearly Defined Mission or Business Purpose

For over two decades, business strategy consultant Dr. Ram Charan has begun his meetings with senior executive teams with two questions: "Where are we now?" and "Where are we taking the business?"

The first question can be answered in many different dimensions such as financial performance, market share, product positioning, technological edge, manufacturing costs, and HR capabilities. But the corporation must also be able to answer, "What is the mission, the purpose, of the organization? What is its reason for being?" To the degree that mission is undefined, the likelihood of optimizing plans for development of key executive resources is lessened. And defining the mission of the organization is fundamental to answering the second question, "Where are we taking the business?"

Supportive Organizational Culture

In the 1980s, consultants and writers had a heyday with corporate culture. Questions were raised such as: "What does 'corporate culture' actually mean?" "How can it be measured or identified?" "Could it be managed or influenced directly?" Many observers have helped us to understand the role culture plays in organizational effectiveness.[1] After a period of popularizing the subject, and then a period during which interest waned, organizations and executives now seem to have settled on the importance of a healthy and supportive corporate culture and its relationship to organizational success.

Core Values and Beliefs   The beliefs and core values held by key executives contribute to the management practices and organizational behaviors that ultimately determine the corporate culture. Thomas J. Watson, Jr., said it well in a speech entitled "A Business and Its Beliefs: The Ideas That Helped Build IBM":

> Consider any great organization—one that has lasted over the years—and I think you will find that it owes its resiliency, not to its form of organization or administrative skills, but to the power of what we call "beliefs" and the appeal these beliefs have for its people. I firmly believe that any organization, in order to survive and achieve success, must have a sound set of beliefs on which it premises all its policies and actions.
>
> Next, I believe that the most important single factor in corporate success is faithful adherence to those beliefs. And finally, I believe that if an organization is to meet the challenges of a changing world, it must be prepared to change everything about itself except those beliefs, as it moves through corporate life.
>
> In other words, the basic philosophy, spirit, and drive of an organization have far more to do with its relative achievements than do technological or

economic resources, organizational structure, innovation and timing. All these things weigh heavily in success. But they are, I think, transcended by how strongly the people in the organization believe in its basic precepts and how faithfully they carry them out.[2]

Responsibility for Setting and Communicating Culture

Good leaders and managers know that an important variable in organizational performance is corporate culture. But determining culture—the core values, the beliefs—cannot be delegated. Stan Davis of Boston University stresses the importance of culture to business success:

> If the CEO ignores culture, he will be formulating strategy without its being grounded in what the company stands for, and he will be attempting to implement it without taking into account the major force for its success or failure. On the other hand, when the CEO works with the culture to strengthen the corporation's strategies, the results can be extraordinarily successful.[3]

Value Statements A corporation's value statement has many implications. For management development, it sets a standard for managers at all levels.

For example, the "Aspirations Statement" for Levi Strauss & Company (Figure 3-1) says much about the company's values. According to Robert Howard, "Many CEOs talk about values, but few have gone to the lengths [Robert D.] Haas [chair and CEO of Levi Strauss] has to bring them to the very center of how he runs the business. The Aspirations Statement is shaping how the company defines occupational roles and responsibilities, conducts performance evaluations, trains new employees, organizes work, and makes business decisions."[4]

The time and energy required to develop a policy document such as the Levi Strauss Aspirations Statement is not inconsequential. And there are many benefits:

1. It has positive impact on the employees. It is a major source of encouragement to see that management actually relies upon the statement for guidance.
2. It not only helps attract good people, but also screens out those who will not fit in.
3. It guides management behavior. Managers know what is expected of them, including the development of people.

FIGURE 3-1
Levi Strauss & Co.—"Aspirations Statement"

We all want a company that our people are proud of and committed to, where all employees have an opportunity to contribute, learn, grow, and advance based on merit, not politics or background. We want our people to feel respected, treated fairly, listened to and involved. Above all, we want satisfaction from accomplishments and friendships, balanced personal and professional lives, and to have fun in our endeavors.

When we describe the kind of Levi Strauss & Co. we want in the future, what we are talking about is building on the foundation we have inherited: affirming the best of our company's traditions, closing gaps that may exist between principles and practices, and updating some of our values to reflect contemporary circumstances.

What type of leadership is necessary to make our Aspirations a Reality?

NEW BEHAVIORS: Leadership that exemplifies directness, openness to influence, commitment to the success of others, willingness to acknowledge our own contributions to problems, personal accountability, teamwork, and trust. Not only must we model these behaviors but we must coach others to adopt them.

DIVERSITY: Leadership that values a diverse work force (age, sex, ethnic group, etc.) at all levels of the organization, diversity in experience, and diversity in perspectives. We have committed to taking full advantage of the rich backgrounds and abilities of all our people and to promoting a greater diversity in positions of influence. Differing points of view will be sought; diversity will be valued and honesty rewarded, not suppressed.

RECOGNITION: Leadership that provides greater recognition—both financial and psychic—for individuals and teams that contribute to our success. Recognition must be given to all who contribute: those who create and innovate and also those who continually support the day-to-day business requirements.

ETHICAL MANAGEMENT PRACTICES: Leadership that epitomizes the stated standards of ethical behavior. We must provide clarity about our expectations and must enforce these standards through the corporation.

COMMUNICATIONS: Leadership that is clear about company, unit, and individual goals and performance. People must know what is expected of them and receive timely, honest feedback on their performance and career aspirations.

EMPOWERMENT: Leadership that increases the authority and responsibility of those closest to our products and customers. By actively pushing responsibilities, trust, and recognition into the organization, we can harness and release the capabilities of all our people.

There is much similarity between value statements that address corporate culture and mission statements that specifically address management development discussed in chapter 5. It should be clear, then, that a statement of corporate beliefs and values that is integrated with beliefs on management development can link management development and strategic planning.

Where employees perceive that the corporation has defined core values and beliefs, succession planning systems will, all other things being equal, be viewed with credibility. Without such credibility, it is virtually impossible to make succession planning work and to link it with the strategic business plan.

Defining Succession Planning as a Strategic Priority

In an interview, Steve McMahon described what he found when he arrived at Fireman's Fund Insurance to be vice president of corporate human resources:

> We had a succession planning program at Fireman's, and one month after I was there, I canceled it. It had been in existence for five years. It was a complete waste of time. It was the joke of the organization; the paper flow started in April and finished in November, and nobody cared.[5]

McMahon went on to say that the program had failed because the senior executives had not bought into it. To use our words, it did not have strategic priority.

Eric Vetter, in describing some of his experiences as vice president for human resources at Gould, Inc., gave us an example of a line manager who demonstrated that succession planning *was* a strategic priority. This particular vice president of operations told Vetter that the most important part of every visit to a plant was the afternoon of the first day he spent with the plant manager, reviewing succession tables and discussing candidates.[6]

In chapter 5, we discuss strategies for gaining corporate commitment to management development or making it a strategic priority. The first strategy is to identify real organizational issues. By identifying current and future business problems, management development may be elevated to its rightful level. Unfortunately, however, because management development has mostly long-term implications, giving it strategic priority may do little to cure short-range problems. In chapter 2 we mentioned the high-tech company that was too busy growing to give management development a strategic priority. Today, that company is going through a change of leadership, its growth has peaked, and it is perceived to have serious problems. Even if the decision were made today to implement a management development system as a high priority, it might be too late.

McMahon also told us how he went about elevating the strategic priority of management development at Fireman's Fund after having found the system in total disarray.

> The Human Resource Advisory Committee came into being by my going to the Chairman and saying that we have a lot of disjointed human resource programs in the company; the times are changing and we have a lot more external forces at work; the workforce is changing; the demographics are changing. We have to take a look at what we have and decide where we want to go in the future. And (I proposed) a group that could work on these issues are the very people that are going to take over the company in the next three to five years.... Over a six month period, this group looked at all the human resource programs in the organization, and they came up with a strategic human resource plan [which included many elements of management development.][7]

The success of this integration was due, in our opinion, to these five basics:

1. The CEO clearly provided sponsorship.
2. Senior-level executives had a vested interest and were involved.
3. There was a clearly defined statement of purpose.
4. Capable staff provided direction and support.
5. The executive was willing to take risks.

Human Resources Must Be "Invited to the Party"

The degree to which senior executives and line management view the HR function with credibility will determine whether or not HR gets "invited to the party."

Many times, HR doesn't get invited. On a recent consulting assignment with a relatively small firm, we observed with amazement over a period of several weeks that the HR director was rarely, if ever, included in the meetings convened by the CEO or division management. This was amazing because the discussions involved organizational restructuring, major cost reduction efforts, and operational improvements that had implications to the size and nature of the workforce. When we questioned his absence, we were told: "Oh, he doesn't get involved in these things until the decisions are made. Then he'll get involved in the implementation; you know, drafting the communications to the employees and working on the separation policies."

For HR management to be able to assist in the development and integration of "people plans," it must be invited to the party! We offer some suggestions to HR managers for making that happen.

Earn Credibility Of course, it is obvious that HR should perform good and useful work. In addition to that, two phrases come to mind: "Be proactive" and "Take risks." Steve McMahon exemplified these qualities in his successful efforts to establish the Human Resource Advisory Committee at Fireman's Fund.

Know the Business One of the prominent consultants in business strategy today has said that, in his opinion, the primary reason that HR activities such as succession planning are not more integrated with business is that the HR people just don't understand the business. Knowing the business means more than just sitting in on business reviews. It means getting out on the shop floor, into the field, and riding in trucks. A good example is Bill Rhoades, employee relations manager (the top HR job) for Monterey Coal Company in Carlinville, Illinois. People who see Bill leave his office in the late afternoon on some days may think his day has ended. But instead, he drives out to the mine to don work clothes, a safety pack, helmet, and lamp to ride down in the elevator with the crew to spend the afternoon shift underground with the workers. It is a practice he has followed for years with all shifts. When Bill meets with line management to discuss employee-related issues, there is no question that he knows the business.[8]

Serve the Client Of course, the client is line management, primarily corporate and divisional. But it is also lower levels of management and the employees. Many HR executives follow the same client contact regimen that any good national accounts representative, business development executive, or bank calling officer would follow to maintain contact with a client. Any good sales representative will tell you that knowing the client's needs is paramount.

Become a Strategic Partner Having HR represented on task forces and special studies is one device for strategic partnering. An example that ties directly to management development is of Tektronix, an Oregon-based electronics instrument manufacturing company.

The Problem: Corporate management felt that its middle management staff was highly proficient technically, but lacked breadth and general management skills. It decided to develop an internal management development program targeted principally at middle managers (managers of managers) and higher. Since a continuing effort to implement a formalized HR planning system had essentially died for lack of a sponsor, this new effort followed a strategy of consensus building and high involvement.

The Strategic Partnering Solution: The CEO and senior management, in response to a proposal submitted by a joint operating and corporate HR team, established two groups of employees and managers to play key roles in the project, which was to develop, on an accelerated basis, several hundred middle managers across the country. The first group was a Human Resources Council comprised of representatives from each operating and staff organization. Its mission was to oversee the project team established to do the actual work. The second group was the Management Steering Group (MSG). Creating this highly respected group of line managers was a crucial step. The six MSG executives were selected based on their companywide credibility, their recognized level (business unit general managers or equivalent), and their representation of a cross section of long service and shorter-term executives. Along with other Tektronix managers whom the MSG selected as highly effective management/leadership models, they were involved in the extensive process of defining what the critical requirements would be for future managers at "Tek." These respected managers went through the process of identifying critical incidents that they had faced in their own work. They then developed a series of management and leadership competencies; the outputs or results expected from Tektronix managers; and the accompanying knowledge, skills, and abilities required. The result was a highly successful middle-management development program. Without the strategic partnering of HR (both the Council and the project team) with the MSG, this program could not have evolved.

Be a Role Model and Advocate for Core Values   Assuming that the CEO has already determined and communicated the values and beliefs of the corporation, HR staff should be the role model and continually assist in defining the values for the organization as needed.

Be a Catalyst for Change   In this book we discuss the need to better adapt management development to the changing business environment. In most cases, HR can be the catalyst for that to happen. Possible needs for change include management skills and training, organization structure, role definition, and even the application of technology to improve employee productivity. Human resources staff can identify the need and suggest responses.

THE FOUR "P's" OF INTEGRATION

As we said at the outset of this chapter, integrating management development with strategic business planning occurs in four different ways: through people, processes, positions, and programs.

People

The primary person involved with management development is the CEO, and it is through him or her that the ultimate linkage of strategic and HR planning takes place. At each lower layer of the organization, linkage occurs where a line manager has responsibility for business direction and the identification and development of executive talent. It is for this reason that we say that line management must have ownership of the management development system. If it is HR management that has that ownership, rather than line management, there will be little linkage with strategic business direction.

Although there is no substitute for the linkage through individuals, a secondary linkage occurs through the interfaces between HR staff and the line management. This occurs when HR participates in joint projects and meetings and works shoulder to shoulder with the line. It is the "strategic partnering" we referred to earlier. The opportunity for this interface was sadly lacking in our example of the HR director who did not participate in the executive meetings on reorganization and downsizing the workforce.

Processes

The management development review process can be integrated with strategic business planning in three ways. The first is to include strategic business issues, such as forecasts of organizational change, on the agenda of management development reviews.

A second way is to have the same executives serve on the management development review committee who sit on the executive committee or other senior-level groups that develop business strategy. For example, at Exxon, the same individuals sit on the Management Committee who sit on the management development review committee.

The third means of integration is to build discussion of "people needs" into each deliberation on projected business opportunities. Such business reviews might include:

- Long-term technology planning sessions
- Research and development reviews
- Acquisition, divestiture, and expansion discussions
- Marketing planning reviews
- Discussions of competition and benchmarking

Not only must the CEO be committed to management development, but he or she must also be committed to linking strategic planning with HR planning. Too often, the CEO creates a barrier instead of a link by purposely excluding HR from critical business discussions with "people" implications.

In our interview with Eric Vetter, we heard this comment on achieving integration through the structured business meetings:

> This kind of structured dialogue among the principals who really matter (when it comes to both business strategies and strategic decisions regarding the development of key people) is one very good way to help assure integration of two organizational practices. Unfortunately, this type of "closely coupled," highly interconnected dialogue, for the value it brings to the organization, based on our consulting experience across a variety of industries, is often missing.[9]

Positions

Using positions and organizational relationships to integrate strategic business and management development decision making is not as obvious (nor probably as important) as the use of people and processes. However, it warrants consideration. Both the job content of the HR positions as well as where the positions are placed in the organization have bearing on the integration. Human resources executives should report to the senior line executive in each division as well as to the CEO at the corporate level to achieve optimum integration. Job descriptions for HR positions that have management development responsibilities can also make a difference. Combining development and training into one position often makes sense. Yet if the training consumes a great deal of short-term involvement (putting on a number of courses, for example), management development will lose out. The executive or manager responsible for management development should have time and the organizational positioning to interact with line management and to support the line's management development activities.

Integration can occur when experienced line executives and managers are assigned to HR positions and also when HR executives are moved into the line. This cross-functional movement is particularly difficult in today's environment, but should not be ruled out. If an organization is large enough to need a full-time executive for management development, an experienced line executive could become easily qualified and would make it possible to integrate business and management development planning through that single position.

Programs

By "programs," we mean developmental or training programs used for the development of managers and executives, both in-house and outside. Management and executive development programming is big business and expensive. According to an article in *Business Week*, an estimated $12 billion is spent annually on all forms of executive development, with slightly more than 25 percent going to business schools.[10] Regrettably, much of this developmental effort may not be linked to business strategies. John Berry, director of executive and organizational development at the Coca Cola Company, listed five reasons why, in his view, management development programs fail to add value to corporate strategy. His first reason is as follows:

> The programs are not linked specifically to the strategies, challenges, or problems of the organization. Instead, the company provides a general course catalog from which managers select courses for themselves or others. Or, managers are asked to predict what kind of training people will need. In neither case are programs linked to the strategies or challenges of the organization.[11]

We recommend that management development programs be specifically selected because of their direct relationship to business. This is not to suggest that a week at the Aspen Institute is not a good investment. But we think that using programs that are business-oriented and bring together executives who can learn from each other about the linkage of people and business planning is more valuable.

We are familiar with one in-house program offered to selected upper-middle managers where development of interpersonal skills is melded into decision making on real business problems that are suggested by the managers themselves. The final session is a visit of the class to the office of the CEO for a no holds barred discussion with only the CEO and the managers present. It is an excellent use of a program to integrate management development with strategic business planning!

MYTHS AND REALITIES

We believe that the linkage of management development with strategic business planning is key to the success of a management development system. But we know that it is not easy. We offer some myths and realities that add to the challenges:

Myth: The integration occurs through a single act.

Reality: There is no single event, whether it be an executive order/memorandum or pronouncement or one single-step process, that will enable the business plan and management development process to be tightly melded. It occurs through a variety of processes and programs. The ultimate integration, however, occurs through people—the values and beliefs they hold and the resulting practices they cause to be put into place. It occurs through the culture they seek to build. It occurs through persistent efforts taken over time to set direction and to get others excited about that direction.

Myth: Executives and managers normally devote great amounts of time, attention, and thought to the "people requirements" inherent in any future business projections.

Reality: In all too many cases, it simply does not happen. Instead the assumption is made that "The people we need will be around. If not, we've always been able to hire what we need, and it won't be a problem again." Human resources practitioners who responded to our survey indicated that competition for senior management's attention to management development is a major concern.

Myth: As division, unit, or subsidiary heads make their annual presentations to the corporate management development committee, they will be able to relate how their management staff fits or complements the business strategy. Thus, they will build the bridge connecting business strategies and the management resources available to implement those strategies.

Reality: It doesn't generally happen, at least in the detail that would leave most objective observers satisfied that a true connection exists between where the business is going and the key resources needed to get there. In many ways, it is a matter of time. The amount of time usually allocated for the senior-level reviews, we have observed, is barely enough to get in all of the needed discussion on people.

CHAPTER CHECK LIST

1. Is there a clearly defined statement of the organization's mission or business purpose?
2. Does the organization's culture play a vital role in:
   a. Support of the business strategy?
   b. The development of managers and executives needed to accomplish the business strategy?
3. Are the organization's core values and beliefs clearly stated and communicated throughout the corporation?
4. Are HR personnel role models for corporate core values?
5. Is management development considered a strategic priority by the CEO and senior management?
6. Does the HR organization have high credibility with senior and line management? Are HR executives regular participants in business discussions involving the workforce?
7. Do HR staff fully understand who their clients are and periodically test to be sure that the clients are being properly served?
8. Is HR a catalyst and champion for change?
9. Do HR staff and executives know the business?
10. Do HR executives seek out opportunities for "strategic partnering" with line managers?
11. Do the CEO and other key line managers have dual responsibility for both strategic planning and management development?

12. Do strategic business planning reviews require executives to report on the HR implications of the business plans, business opportunities, new products, or changes in organization?

13. Do the management development reviews include information on the forecast business initiatives with major HR implications?

14. Is management development linked to strategic business planning in the management development reviews at all levels?

15. Are line managers ever considered for filling the HR staff position that directs the management development process?

16. Is HR properly positioned in the organization?

17. Are management development and training programs designed to integrate business strategies with interpersonal and other managerial skills?

Negative answers to any of these questions should identify target areas for developing better integration of management development and strategic decision making. We hope that practical suggestions will be found in sections II and III of this book.

Chapter Four

LESSONS FROM JAPAN

W e asked ourselves whether Japan has changed our perspective on management development and whether we should devote a chapter in this book to Japan. The answer came early in 1992 when President Bush and a delegation of American business leaders visited Tokyo and set off a heated debate concerning trade with that nation. In response to charges that the Japanese were treating America unfairly, Japanese Parliament House Speaker Yoshio Sakurauchi said: "The quality of American labor is poor. About 30 percent of the workers cannot read. Under these circumstances, executives cannot give [them] written instructions."[1]

This brought further explanation a week later by Shintaro Ishihara, co-author of *The Japan That Can Say No*: "[Sakurauchi] should have said the quality of American business managers is inferior. U.S. management is no good. I guess it is a cultural difference."[2] Ishihara, an ardent nationalist and longtime critic of Japan's efforts to secure good working relationships with the United States, set into motion more heated debate with his indictment of America's management competence.

We feel that it is both important and timely to examine some of the differences in management development between the two countries. It is because our competition with Japan is very real that we should not neglect an examination of its practices. In a few decades, Japan has become *the* formidable global competitor for the United States and the rest of the Western world. Its financial clout, technology, manufacturing techniques, and national work ethic have combined to produce an indisputable and immeasurable 20th-century success story. While some of the human resources practices employed by Japanese companies are to be neither recommended nor admired, some certain practices related to employee selection, training, and management development have contributed greatly to Japan's success. We will examine some of these in this chapter.

SELECTING AND HIRING THE BEST

Clyde V. Prestowitz, Jr., has thoughtfully compared American and Japanese ways in *Trading Places*. He comments on selection and hiring:

> Superficially, the hiring process appears to be similar in U.S. and Japanese companies. In fact, nothing could be more different. The U.S. company is hiring a new employee. The Japanese company is adopting a new member into the family. The first kind of obligation is contractual; the second, intensely personal.[3]

Prestowitz describes a very different philosophy, a different mind-set, that guides the hiring process followed by Japanese companies versus the attitudes that tend to govern the hiring process in U.S. companies. Of the many aspects of the management development process, none is more important than selecting the right candidates for employment. To use an old processing-industry term, it is selecting the "feedstock" (the raw material being fed into the process).

It would be wrong to suggest that Hewlett-Packard, IBM, Exxon, GE, or many other U.S. corporations hire only to fill vacant positions. Indeed, many firms attempt to hire people with both the aspiration and potential to advance much higher in the organization and who are oriented toward long-term employment. But even among highly respected firms, few seem to approach the new hire with the same set of beliefs or paternalistic fervor as do the Japanese.

Selective Hiring

The Japanese attitude toward the employment process has surfaced in recruiting practices for some of the auto assembly plants being constructed in the United States. Some observers maintain that the objective is to select employees who will not be prone to union organization. Yet, Mazda, unlike Nissan and Honda, began negotiations with United Auto Workers even before employees had been hired, and it has attempted to include the union's leadership as part of its team.[4]

The reasons that Japanese companies take such great care in selecting employees are much deeper than to thwart union organization. Certainly, a principal objective is to hire employees who will stay committed to the vision and goals of the company for the long term. The Japanese consider future potential and learning ability to be far more important than entry skills and will invest heavily in training to impart the needed skills. C. Jackson Grayson, Jr., and Carla O'Dell have written about the Nissan plant in Smyrna, Tennessee, which started up with less than 20 percent of the employees having any prior experience in building automobiles. According to Grayson and O'Dell, "That lack of experience was offset by careful selection for learning skills and tremendous training—about $60 million worth before start-up."[5] The point is that the Japanese select and hire each employee with the expectation that a full career is ahead, while U.S. employers tend to hire based on existing qualifications and count on normal processes of attrition and competition to weed out misfits.

In comparison to U.S. firms, most Japanese companies place a far greater emphasis on the selection process. Robert L. Shook describes the process used by Honda for its U.S. plants in *Honda: An American Success Story:* "While HAM [Honda of America Manufacturing Inc.] does not have a lifetime employment policy like Japanese Honda and like many other companies in Japan, its recruiters sought people for long-term employment. Accepting personnel turnover is a poor way to conduct business; it is both costly and demoralizing."[6] The care in selection is not because of a shortage of applicants. For example, at one Honda plant in the United States, the ratio of applicants to hires was 40 to 1.[7]

The Japanese Selection Model

Joseph I. and Suzi Fucini describe the employee selection process used for the new Mazda plant that went into full production in 1988 at Flat Rock, Michigan. In *Working for the Japanese*, they discuss the five selection steps, which, in addition to the application, include a battery of tests, personal interviews, group problem solving in an assessment center, and simulated work exercises.[8] The Fucinis write that Mazda needed to hire people who not only knew how to express their own ideas but who could also get along with others and resolve their differences constructively. They further state that Mazda's emphasis on cross-training and job rotation created a need for workers who were intelligent enough to learn a variety of jobs and flexible enough to adjust to a work routine that had no rigid job classifications.[9] However, the specific selection techniques used by Japanese manufacturers is not the point here. What is important is that the Japanese invest more in the front-end selection process than do most American companies.

Although the Japanese selection model has many positive attributes, there are downsides to a selection process that is geared to full career employment and also intended to maximize retention. The downsides include the cost of the selection process itself. It takes time, resources, and a management committed to the process. Often both the employer and the employee are reluctant to agree to an early termination when a mismatch has occurred, even though it may be mutually beneficial. Thus, some employees remain on the job who should be terminated. Another downside is that the employee's feeling of security breeds complacency.

However, the benefits of the system used by the Japanese can outweigh the negatives. Employees will be hired who are better matched to the culture, needs, and objectives of the organization, thus assuring a higher degree of personal commitment, positive attitude, and improved customer service. Employee turnover, with its direct and indirect costs, will be reduced. There will likely be a greater return on the investment made in training and education of employees. Perhaps the greatest benefit of all comes from the demonstration of the value the company places on each employee. This display of respect has positive impact on each aspect of employee relations. It is the first step in building a genuine and lasting bond between the organization and the employee.

COMMITMENT TO LEARNING

Lifetime Learning

Japan's greatest long-term comparative advantage . . . is the Japanese commitment to learning.

C. Jackson Grayson, Jr., and Carla O'Dell[10]

Japan is far ahead in education on three counts: (1) it has set exceptionally high standards for education; (2) it has a system to provide education; and (3) students and their parents *want* education. We note that this last point may represent the biggest challenge for education in the United States.

The education system in Japan is not without problems. It is a system that exudes competitiveness beginning with the earliest years of a student's educational experience. Many people believe that contributes heavily to the unsettling rate of suicide by high school students. Japanese teachers tend to emphasize written examinations, a quality that no doubt contributes to students' competency in math and science. However, some people believe that this emphasis causes Japanese students to have difficulty in learning to speak English. Other people point out that the few Nobel Prize winners from Japan as compared with those from the United States indicates that the Japanese system does not promote creativity and conceptual thinking. These weaknesses may be real, but in our opinion they are far outweighed by the benefits of the commitment to learning.

The importance of learning is endemic to the Japanese culture. For example, the regular school year in Japan is 240 days compared to about 180 days in the United States.[11] There are countless other statistics—hours per day of class, hours of homework, time spent reading—that suggest that Japanese students take learning more seriously than do their American counterparts. Rosalie L. Tung sums up the differences in *Key to Japan's Economic Strength: Human Power:* "The average high school graduate in Japan receives an equivalent of four more years of education than his or her American counterpart."[12] Thus, it is easy to understand how and why Japanese firms continue to emphasize education for their employees.

America's Response

America's relative deficiency in education has not gone unnoticed, although we are late in addressing it. Lamar Alexander, U.S. Secretary of Education, has set six ambitious National Education Goals to be achieved by the Year 2000:

- All American children will start school each day ready to learn.
- The high school graduation rate will increase to at least 90 percent.
- Students will leave grades 4, 8, and 12 having demonstrated competency in challenging subject matter.
- American students will be the first in the world in science and mathematics.
- Every adult will be literate and will possess knowledge and skills necessary to compete in a global economy.
- Every school will be free of drugs and violence and will offer a disciplined environment conducive to learning.[13]

Quite naturally, these words are received with skepticism by the typical inner-city public school teacher. But, finally, as a nation, we are talking about the problems of public education and relating them to the issue of our ability to compete with the rest of the world.

How strongly do Japanese corporations feel about training? Robert Shook says of HAM: "Hundreds of new associates [employees] were sent to Honda's headquarters and plants in Japan, sometimes within a couple of weeks or months of joining the company. These trips were designed primarily to introduce new people to Honda's technological and managerial methods so they could be implemented at HAM."[14] And Martin K. Starr, Director for the Center for Operations of the Columbia Graduate School of Business, comments: "The training (and cross training) of employees is crucial to the success of Japanese manufacturers in Tennessee. . . . Because of high employee turnover, U.S. managers tend to limit investments in training. Japanese investments are about three times greater."[15] There are certainly examples of corporate dedication to education in U.S. companies. But in total, the American corporate commitment to training does not compare favorably with that of the Japanese.

Too many U.S. companies give only lip service to training. Some American corporations will sacrifice training during the first phase of a budget cut. Also, in this country there is a tendency to put full responsibility for training on the HR staff. Human resources personnel can design and administer training programs. But line management must demonstrate its full commitment to and involvement in the program, something that the Japanese appear to do better.

In Japan, the corporate emphasis on education seems to focus on broadening the employee rather than just on skills training. This leads appropriately to the discussion of job rotation, a form of education much used by the Japanese.

JOB ROTATION

The Japanese strongly believe that a good manager specializes more in the company than in a particular discipline.

C. Jackson Grayson and Carla O'Dell[16]

The practice of developing careers through work exposure to many functions is an area of management development on which the Japanese place great emphasis. In the United States, we talk a lot about job rotation and multifunctional exposure, but in practice it is not easy to achieve. In this country, in a spirit of decentralized authority, it is difficult to force a department manager or a division head to take an employee from another department and train him or her in a new function. It seems to go against the accountability and responsibility inherent in decentralization.

Grayson and O'Dell point out:

> Top executives in the fifty largest American firms have worked in fewer than two functions on their way up the corporate ladder. . . . [In Japan] while climbing the seniority ladder, an employee might hold widely different positions in different functions, with each posting usually lasting no more than three years. . . . A Japanese manager ends up with somewhat less specialized knowledge (which would be obsolete in five years anyway) and a much more integrated and personal knowledge of the organization.[17]

It would appear that the Japanese are far ahead of us in producing an environment that both accepts and practices job rotation. Call it culture, if you will, but employees are used to and accept their career progress as planned by the employer. Job rotation then becomes a mutually desired goal of employee and employer alike. For many U.S. companies there is a mutual aversion to job rotation, particularly if the move is interfunctional. Managers see less advantage to themselves in moving employees into new experiences just for training. On the other hand, employees are impatient about their own advancement and therefore reluctant to accept lateral moves. Where the moves are interfunctional (manufacturing to marketing, for example), the aversion may be even greater. For interfunctional moves to work, there must be a strong commitment and support from the senior management.

We concede that there are practical limitations to functional job rotation in the United States. Because of the strain such moves place on an organization (in our culture), we see such moves being limited to very high potential candidates who are being groomed for the highest levels of general management. However, we would encourage a greater use of job rotation within functions to provide growth to employees.

LIFETIME EMPLOYMENT

A common expression used to describe Japanese corporate culture is "lifetime employment." The term, while partly accurate (to the segment of the workforce to which it applies), is misleading. Grayson and O'Dell point out that job security in Japanese companies lasts only to age 55–60 and that only 25 to 33 percent of the Japanese workers benefit from it.[18] (And it largely excludes women.) Still, there is a degree of employment stability that exceeds that in most U.S. corporations. Certainly "promotion from within," a phrase that companies in the West easily understand, would accurately describe the Japanese system.

Clyde Prestowitz has keen insight into the Japanese culture when he says: "The Japanese see as very strange the U.S. practice of hiring people from outside to fill key senior positions. They wonder how such executives can understand the way of thinking of their new [corporate] families without having grown up in them, without having been a member from the start."[19] According to Prestowitz, in the Japanese company most advancement is by seniority. The Japanese apparently believe that the seniority system encourages the employee to both participate more as a team member than as a competitor and accept rotational assignments in a spirit of learning without concern about career advancement.

In *Theory Z*, William G. Ouchi describes the career path of a graduate of the University of Tokyo in a fictional major bank. For the first 10 years, the graduate will receive the same promotions and pay increases as the other 15 employees who were hired at the same time. It will be only after 10 years that an evaluation takes place, and then promotions will be based on merit.[20] In this scenario it is easy to see how the employee can attend to learning and performing to his or her best without worrying about the next promotion or career progression.

Contrast that scenario with American corporations' efforts over the past two decades, to eradicate the idea that promotion is based largely on seniority. (Let's hope we stick to our system on that issue.) Our entire system of enterprise is premised on the belief that competition is healthy and that there are ways of channeling the competitive spirit into productive team participation. The very real cultural differences between the United States and Japan notwithstanding would suggest that Japan is moving (albeit slowly) to a more Western practice of "performance based promotions."[21]

There are many U.S. corporations that have tried for years to live by a full employment policy. IBM, Hewlett-Packard, Tektronix, Kollmorgan, and Hallmark are examples. Generally having a full employment policy means that the employer will do everything in its power to prevent layoffs. It does not mean that each employee is guaranteed a job for life, but it certainly provides for greater peace of mind.

Hallmark Cards has enjoyed a reputation for employee benevolence since its founding in 1910. Several years ago, President and CEO Irvine Hockaday described his company's efforts in the face of increasingly stiff competition, margin pressure from retailers, and slow industry growth. He said, "We believe that we have to manage for the long term, protect our people from cyclical, changing markets, and if they know we are going to do that, they will help us solve the problem."[22] (We like the suggestion that the employees can help in solving the problem, something executives often fail to recognize!)

Obviously a corporation must see clear long-term benefits to take such a stand, and no doubt IBM, Hewlett-Packard, Hallmark Cards, and other firms have. Many corporations, unfortunately, have neither the size nor stability to make such a commitment. For those who do, it is amazing how many options can be uncovered—retraining, relocation, sweetened voluntary separations or retirements—in order to make it possible. The benefits are often difficult to measure with accuracy, and the out-of-pocket costs are real. Some of the benefits relate to the quality and retention of human resources, and, at least for the long term, these benefits are well worth trying to achieve.

It is interesting that major Japanese corporations locating facilities in the United States seem not to be bringing along with them a policy of lifetime employment.

The Japanese approach to lifetime employment is not without its problems. In Japan, lifetime employment is more a matter of culture than of management decisions. It is an extreme that can produce some harmful side effects:

- The employee is trapped. Employees feel trapped when they are limited to a single corporation for their careers. Conversely, individual motivation and creativity are enhanced when employees are free to change employers when the opportunity arises for them to increase their level of contribution. The Japanese system, in its extreme, is akin to indentured servitude.

- Paternalism (or control) breeds complacency. The bureaucracy we call government seems to suffer from this disease. Although the success of many Japanese corporations would suggest that complacency is not a problem, it can manifest itself in many ways, such as an unwillingness to take risk or to try new approaches.

- It burdens the selection process. The American way of hiring for some attrition allows for the selection of employees who do not fit any one mold, which tends to build healthier organizations. Employees will recognize a mismatch early enough in their careers to make a new start elsewhere. The Japanese employee tends to be locked in, even when a mismatch has occurred. To put it another way, a rigid lifetime employment system does not provide for the correction of mistakes on hiring, whether those mistakes were made by the employee or by the corporation.

There is a middle ground. As with most of the practices we discuss, there are few clear demarcations but different shades of application. The extremes on the continuum of lifetime employment are:

INDIVIDUAL ENTREPRENEURSHIP → LIFETIME EMPLOYMENT

Japanese companies are, of course, at the far right (for a substantial percentage of their workforce). The far left position reflects a philosophy that each employee stands alone with no long-term commitment either to or from an employer. We believe the better position is closer to the middle. The system should provide the potential for, not the guarantee of, lifetime employment while not preventing opportunity elsewhere. A strong "promote from within" philosophy can provide the foundation for such a system and should provide sufficient career growth opportunities so that an adequate supply of high-potential candidates can be groomed for senior management positions without the need to recruit executives from the outside.

VISION

The look-ahead of Americans is 10 minutes versus 10 years for the Japanese.

Akio Morito (cofounder and chair of Sony Corporation) and Shintaro Ishihara.[23]

Kenji Yoshizawa, head of the Bank of Tokyo's Western Hemisphere operations, responded to that statement in *Management Review*: "Comparing 10 minutes to 10 years is an overstatement, but there is some truth in the criticism. From an outsider's point of view, it is quite visible that American management tend to think in rather short terms."[24] Yoshizawa is even kinder toward us. He believes that some of our focus on the short term keeps us more alert to day-to-day changes in operations. He says that there are merits and demerits in both systems, the statement of a true diplomat.

The challenge for U.S. industry is to apply longer-range thinking in its decision making. It must not be to the total exclusion of assessing the short term, particularly as it relates to decisions affecting management and executive resources. According to Rosalie Tung, the higher growth rate in productivity among Japanese companies can be attributed largely to the longer perspective adopted by their executives.[25] This attention to the longer perspective is popularly labeled "vision." And clearly, Japanese executives seem to exhibit a far stronger orientation to it than their American counterparts.

The reasons for the apparent high level of corporate vision by the Japanese are varied. Japanese executives do not feel the hot breath of investors and analysts ready to jump ship at an unsatisfactory quarterly report. They may believe that their government will support them in a longer-term focus. In a very real way, the powerful Ministry of Industry and Trade (MITI), Japan's banking system, and the industrial cartels (*keiretsu*) are conducive to a longer-term focus. And possibly the culture and homogeneity of the Japanese people produces less internal competition and a greater degree of patience.

But for whatever reasons, Japanese executives, as a group, seem far more apt to make decisions based on their long-range impact than are their American counterparts. This tendency has great significance in management development in that employees are selected, trained, and developed based on long-term needs, not on short-term, bottom-line results.

Being concerned about the survival of the entity is a subset of having vision. Many American executives and investors tend to value their own contribution to the corporation in immediate dollars, not in assuring corporate survival. This school of thought is well illustrated by the LBO-crazed, junk-bond financing schemes of the 1980s and the "sell assets to service debt" mentality. "If selling the entity produces better financial results now, do it!" Certainly, if employees sense that their company or division is always vulnerable to a decision to sell or dissolve, they will demonstrate their insecurity in their performance and have little interest in a management development system. Japanese corporations, because of the many differences in their culture, do not appear to have this problem.

PROBLEMS FACING JAPANESE MANAGEMENT

*A look under the kimono reveals a world where many Japanese
managers see their own lives beset by institutional rigidity, murderous
competition and, in recent years, rapidly diminishing expectations.*

Joel Kotkin and Yoriko Kishimoto[26]

Even in Japan, life can be a struggle. Applying vision to the rigid Japanese
corporate system for human resources and management development shows
that some cracks in the armor are beginning to develop. For instance,
Japanese people appear to be growing disenchanted with their standard of
living. Life is more of a struggle for the average Japanese person than we
might assume for a citizen in an affluent and successful society. Working
hours are long, particularly when required socializing in the evening is
added to the workday hours in the office or plant. Living and recreational
space is limited. Commitment to the corporation requires major personal
sacrifice. To the Japanese, the word *karoshi*—death by overwork—has literal
meaning. Many question whether the populace will continue to blindly
accept a system in which the individual has so little control over his or her
destiny.

Even for those who benefit from the security of "lifetime employment,"
opportunities for advancement are becoming fewer and societal and cultural
mores make it very difficult to change employers to realize self-improve-
ment. This limitation has heightened the level of employee dissatisfaction
and created increased pressures among employees for change.

Joel Kotkin and Yoriko Kishimoto, authors of *The Third Century—America's Resurgence in the Asian Era,* paint a different picture from what has
been the party line from many Japan watchers. Kotkin and Kishimoto point
out that Japan's low rate of employee turnover—about half the American
rate during the first five years on the job—reflects not so much the intense
organizational loyalty as a distinct lack of alternatives.[27] They illustrate that
the old management system and the traditional loyalty structure in Japan
are breaking down, particularly among the young.

There is a growing shortage of Japanese workers. Just as in the United
States, the demographics of the Japanese workforce are changing. The

workforce is graying at an even greater rate than in America. According to Thomas R. Horton, former chair and CEO of The American Management Association, by the Year 2001 almost 16 percent of Japan's population will be over age 65, versus less than 13 percent in the United States.[28]

In a Nippon Hoso Kyokai survey of Japanese executives conducted for *Business Week* in 1990, 72 percent of the executives surveyed indicated that a labor shortage and the aging of the workforce would be the most important factor in holding back Japan's economic growth in the 1990s.[29] Fewer Japanese workers will be supporting more retirees, a problem that has a familiar ring.

Because of the tight market for labor, recruiting will be moving from a buyer's market to a seller's market for the Japanese. With fewer qualified candidates to fill jobs, search firms are beginning to appear on the Japanese scene. Jenny C. McCune has discussed the growing shortage of workers. She points out that filling entry-level spots is becoming more difficult, particularly for jobs requiring a college education. She states that Japan, king of consumer electronics, doesn't have enough engineers graduating from college. McCune mentions a new category of Japanese—"mid-term employees"—who are hired away from other companies. She says that Seiko-Epson Corp. hired 300 mid-termers in 1990 as compared to only 100 in 1987.[30]

Women are not being utilized. Some of what has been written about Japan would have the Western world believing that Japanese women are not interested in combining professional careers with motherhood. A similar argument was being made 20 years ago in this country to explain why there were so few women in professional and managerial jobs. Just as we have seen a drastic change in the United States in the past 20 years, we predict that the attitudes and practices concerning the role of women in Japan will be undergoing considerable change in coming years.

John E. Rehfeld's experience—eight years as vice president and general manager of Toshiba America's computer business and now president and chief operating officer of Seiko Instruments USA Inc.—has enabled him to make an objective and credible evaluation of this issue. While his comments toward Japanese management style are very favorable, he regards Japanese managers' attitudes toward women as a blind spot. He says:

Japanese companies are unwilling to invest in training their female employees. As a result, this highly educated part of the work force is terribly underused.

I've often seen very competent women who have graduated from the top universities do little more than serve tea. In the 15 years I've been closely involved with Japanese companies, most of the "career moves" I've seen women make are to graduate slowly from tea servers to note takers to administrative assistants.[31]

Rehfeld traces this to the custom of Japanese women's leaving the workforce at about age 25 to raise their families. The culture does not support their return to work. Therefore an investment in training for women is perceived as a poor one. In a more critical vein, William Ouchi notes that there is probably no form of organization more sexist or racist than the Japanese corporation.[32]

Dealing with nonnationals brings some new challenges to the Japanese. John Rehfeld refers to another Japanese blind spot—outsiders. He describes the strong old boy network in each company that makes it hard for outsiders to be accepted.[33] In the area of bias and discrimination, the Japanese would be well advised to study U.S. history, since they appear to be more than a generation behind us. The Japanese people themselves, the foreign employees upon whom they must depend, and their global customers may not tolerate their insensitivity much longer.

The Japanese employee who goes global will bring home some new ideas. Possibly the greatest impact of Japan's globalization (as far as management development is concerned) comes from the number of Japanese who are given the opportunity to work and live in foreign lands and different cultures (such as the United States, where individuality is both tolerated and encouraged and where freedom of choice is a primary attribute). When these young managers return home to positions in Japan, they will be bringing back new ideas and demands concerning opportunity and the freedom to change employers. The ideas that employees, their spouses, and children will have developed through educational systems, interacting with neighbors, and interacting with fellow workers, will inevitably have impact on the Japanese corporation. It will not be surprising, then, that the Japanese closed system for employment—"in at entry level and thereafter at the discretion of the company"—will likely change. If Japan wishes to examine the implications of this change, it need only study the changes that have already occurred in the United States with regard to management development. And as the Japanese people begin to express themselves to a greater degree as individuals, they will become less likely to accept the collective thinking for the common good of the corporation as is now imposed on them.

Osamu Nobuto, an executive sent to America to head up Mazda's manufacturing venture, spoke tellingly in an interview with the *Detroit News:* "Of course becoming part of the Mazda team means much more than donning the company uniform and participating in morning calisthenics. It also means conforming to a group way of thinking, of not only doing what one is told but of wanting to do what one is told."[34]

We doubt that the Japanese people are really satisfied to let someone else think for them. As they learn more about societies in the rest of the world, they are likely to become more inclined to express themselves as individuals.

HOW DOES THE UNITED STATES COMPARE?

Many books have been written about the modern Japanese management style and the Japanese corporation, yet it is difficult to fully understand, evaluate, and compare Japanese management development systems. Although there is still much to be learned, we offer the following comparisons of Japan with the United States.

1. Japan has an edge in selection. Management development can succeed only with the selection of the right employees. Candidates should be considered on the basis of their potential for long careers and not just for entry-level jobs. The care taken by the Japanese in the selection of the right individual is a practice to be emulated. To be sure, some U.S. employers closely follow the Japanese model. However, a selection process that is so rigid as to produce total uniformity (the Japanese way) is not as desirable as one that brings in a heterogeneous group of new hires, each with his or her own ideas, creativity, and uniqueness who are given encouragement to express their individuality.

2. Japan is ahead in the emphasis on learning. The Japanese have a considerable edge in the emphasis on education and training, which has positive implications for management development. The fact that continuing learning and lifetime learning are so strongly entrenched in the Japanese culture gives the Japanese a clear advantage in the development and growth of all employees, including executives. Most American companies have a long way to go in changing management's commitment to the "continuing learning" philosophy.

3. Lifetime employment in Japan will become limited to fewer employees. However, if the Japanese continue to encourage employees

to follow one-company careers and, more importantly, practice promotion from within, they should build stronger management. Japanese corporations lose some of this advantage by having a rigid system that gives employees practically no option but to stay with their first employer.

4. The issue of "long view" versus "immediate bottom line" is one of extremes. It is impossible for responsible U.S executives to ignore the quarterly results. Our system demands it. Yet the Japanese appear to have a clear advantage with a system that encourages longer-range, investment-oriented decision making. For U.S. corporations in a results-oriented culture, more vision in the development of people will be moving in the right direction.

5. The Japanese must learn from us in dealing with a dynamic workforce. As the workforce ages and the shortage of qualified applicants increases, younger Japanese employees will be more willing and will have more opportunity to change employers to enhance their careers. Corporate management in Japan will have to adjust to the changing dynamics. Our system is presently superior to the Japanese system in this regard.

6. The United States is far ahead of Japan in recognizing the individual's right to freedom of thought, expression, and choice. This is clearly an advantage for the United States in its continuing competition with Japan for global markets. It is a fairly safe bet that Japan will learn that "individuality," when properly directed, is a great strength.

7. As we will discuss in chapter 8, the concept of workforce diversity has not been an easy concept for many managers in the United States to accept. Great progress has been made, but there is no question that we have a long way to go. By comparison, Japan considers its homogeneity as a strength. Just as we in the United States were slow to see the value of diversity, so have the Japanese failed to recognize it. But if and when the Japanese accept diversity as a strength, they will simply become stronger.

It would be naive to believe that the success of Japan Inc. is because of its emphasis on employee selection, learning, promotion from within, or on greater vision. There are many other variables that contribute to Japan's success—cheap capital, the cooperative advantage of *keiretsu*, and a supportive government, to name a few.

We cannot and would not seek to duplicate the Japanese culture. It is built on homogeneity, whereas the roots of our culture are heterogeneous. Ours is a mixture of races and ethnic backgrounds, a world melting pot, that is perceived by many to be the very strength of our nation. We *are* a nation of diversity. It may make the job of developing managers more difficult, but we can surely rise to the challenge.

The Japanese have been successful in using certain practices that enable or enhance the management development process. Similarly, those practices cannot and should not be adopted wholesale. There are practices that can enhance management development if applied by American business and industry. Conversely, the Japanese stand to learn much from us in the area of individuality and managing within a diverse culture.

If we were forced to choose between one system or the other, the Japanese system would be a step backward. If we apply to our system those concepts of Japanese management that recognize the individual human resources as long-term corporate investments, we will move forward.

ELEMENTS OF AN EFFECTIVE MANAGEMENT DEVELOPMENT SYSTEM

Chapter Five

THE CRITICAL NEED FOR CORPORATE COMMITMENT

W e asked Eric Vetter, a standard bearer for succession planning, what he saw as the main reasons succession planning systems fail. His response reinforces the importance of senior management's commitment. Vetter said: "I think the key reason [for failure of a succession planning system] is that the top of the organization is not committed to it. . . . And Human Resources people make classic mistakes when they try to get a system going and keep trying to force it to run when the key people in management don't want it."[1]

In this chapter we will examine the issue of corporate commitment, some of the reasons it is difficult to generate, and what practitioners can do to overcome the barriers to commitment.

MISSION AND PURPOSE

As with all business strategies, there must be a mission. In our interviews with HR executives and succession planning practitioners, we have heard "mission" defined in a variety of ways. For some it is a simple statement. According to Walter R. Trosin, vice president for human resources for Merck, "Simply stated, the principal mission of our program is to assure that we have a consistent flow of high-quality executive talent."[2]

We would define the mission of management succession planning, or management development system as we prefer to describe it, as twofold: It is to assure a continuous supply of competent managers and executives, in the quantity and quality needed at just the right time, and it is to assure individual growth in fulfilling that business need.

The process is not just something done *to* individuals but rather a series of steps in a continuous and integrated management development effort. From the individual's perspective, it addresses motives, personal goals, talents, experience, potential, and ongoing developmental needs. From the organization's perspective, it addresses core values, business goals and objectives, and present and future organization structure.

The mission of a management development system is achieved through the performance of several activities:

- Recruiting and early training of qualified people
- Assessing individual performance and potential continuously at all levels
- Determining and implementing career paths that will provide needed growth experiences
- Determining long-range supply/demand balances for managerial resources
- Training and developing individuals with internal and external programs
- Delegating responsibilities for the development process involving individuals
- Involving senior management in understanding and committing resources to the development plans for employees with high potential
- Holding department and corporate level reviews of high-potential individuals along with review of their development plans
- Holding senior-level reviews of specific plans as well as of the planning process itself

A well-integrated system will involve a series of HR support activities as well as the decision making by line management. It is a team effort. Neither HR staff nor line management can fulfill the mission alone.

Although these activities may seem to be addressed largely from the perspective of the organization, the focus remains on the individual. An important and often-stated goal of successful companies, from the time of the earliest management development systems, has been to achieve the growth of an *individual* to his or her highest potential. It is not trite to say that the real strength of a company is its people!

POLICY AND PRACTICE

In the traditional corporate culture, policy manuals often become simply the tools of the audit staff. In many companies, written policy statements are consulted only when it is necessary to take disciplinary or other action. Then, policies are reviewed by line management to ensure compliance when difficult decisions must be made. Measuring behavior against policy quite frequently is used to determine the nature of the violation for the purpose of discipline. In the worst cases, policy becomes the law of the corporation rather than guidelines for management and employees.

Our idea of a useful policy is a statement that is clear and can help all facets of an organization work toward a common goal. The statement of goals of the relatively new corporation, Perot Systems,[3] struck us as a form of policy that will be understood at all levels. Included are statements such as these:

We will—

- Have only one class of team member—each member will be a full partner.
- Recognize and reward effort while the individual is still sweating from his efforts.
- Build and maintain a spirit of "one for all and all for one."
- Eliminate any opportunity for people to succeed by merely "looking good."
- Promote solely on merit.

Policy is the common thread for executive development. Despite the current advice to get rid of the policy manuals and the movement toward reducing the number of guidelines that constrain organizations' competitiveness, a written policy statement can play a very positive role in management development. It can be used to convey: the spirit of commitment from the senior executives; the recommended guidelines for line management; the guideline for implementation and a monitoring tool for HR staff; and just as importantly, the communications to employees and potential employees. It can become the common thread that ties together the involvement of senior executives, middle management, HR staff, and employees.

An important first step for installing a management development system is the implementation of a written corporate policy. The statement should be the product of a senior management group that has spent time in serious discussion. Human resources staff can provide much of the research and can develop external benchmarks from organizations that senior management considers credible and worthy. But, in the final analysis, it is senior management that must be willing to declare what it believes, what it expects, and what it will do.

Keep It Simple

The statement of goals for Perot Systems is an example of how a philosophy and commitment can be stated clearly and simply. Ross Perot let his eight cofounders shape the statement of goals for his new corporation. That statement is not a nuts and bolts set of procedures. But it is a clear commitment from senior management that can be understood and by which the managers and employees can measure themselves. Such a set of beliefs could easily serve as a first step in the design and implementation of an effective management development system.

The policy statement on management development for a corporation should be *unique* to that organization, and it should be *simple*. The language must reflect the corporate culture, the point in time of the establishment of the management development process, and the management style of the senior executives. The executive memorandum reproduced at Figure 5-1 was used by the chair of a large corporation launching an executive succession planning and development process. It does not give detailed procedures. Rather it expresses need, objectives, and corporate commitment. This kind of statement must be augmented by specific procedures. But if the policy statement is clear, it can become the framework for an entire management development system.

What to Address

The written policy should address these key points:

- Need: The importance of the growth and development of each individual employee
- Corporate commitment
- A clear philosophy: the desire to promote from within as much as possible
- Accountability: The responsibility of line managers for the growth and development of their employees

- Process: The system for review and stewardship of management development.

FIGURE 5-1
Executive Memorandum

It has been evident for some time that we need to place a greater emphasis on planning for management and executive continuity. A more unified process must be followed if we are to achieve the most effective integration and direction of our increasing worldwide operations. The need for competent professional managers in our company has never been greater. While we do not expect spectacular overnight results, we are committed to substantial near-term improvements. The desired changes and improvements will occur only to the degree that management is dedicated to this achievement.

While we have in the past regularly addressed management continuity needs, this program is designed to achieve several new objectives as well as to refine some of the old. These include:

(a) Identification and development of executives capable of assuming a variety of assignments at successive management levels

(b) Fuller utilization of the developmental capacity and opportunities which currently exist within the company

(c) Planned manager exchange between organizations of the company which will result in a more broadly experienced, flexible management group

(d) Increased ability to provide career advancement opportunities for female and minority employees

(e) Clearer focus on individual development needs to ensure the optimum return on developmental investments

For this program to succeed, it is absolutely essential that all key managers give it top priority with frequent personal review to ensure needed progress.

In *The Leadership Factor,*[4] John Kotter writes that the largest of the "Best Practices" firms tend to have some formal policy designed to support sound development practices. He uses General Electric's Development Philosophy, created in the mid-1970s, as an example. We reproduce 5 of the 10 key policy statements here:

- Assuring development of managerial excellence in the company is the chief executive's most important responsibility.

- Managers at all layers must be similarly responsible and must "own" the development system(s).
- Promotion from within—for its motivational value—will be the rule, not the exception.
- A key step in planning the development of managers is the . . . review process.
- Staff people must add value in these processes, but their roles are secondary to the managerial roles.

GE firmly fixes responsibility with the CEO and all line managers and defines HR's role. It establishes the review process and commits to the entire organization a policy of promotion from within to the extent possible.

In *A Great Place to Work*, Robert Levering lists the employee rights at Marion Labs. The list includes: "Each associate has the right to . . . share in the growth of the company through personal and career growth."[5] It's not an insignificant statement. It places a corporate focus on employee development, but more importantly, it does it by making a commitment to employees. It may not be a complete policy, but it can lay the foundation for a management development system.

Of course, written policy is meaningless if the words don't translate into action. But without a written statement, a viable developmental system is not likely to exist or operate. With management's commitment, an explicit policy can be an effective communications tool and a standard by which to measure management's actions.

COMMITMENT OF SENIOR MANAGEMENT

Succession planning practitioners agree that the commitment of senior management is essential to a viable management development system. And many would agree that genuine commitment, not lip service, is difficult to obtain. We might ask why CEOs are not fully committed when a company as successful as GE says that the development of managerial excellence is the CEO's most important responsibility. Many reasons are given, but most of them are weak and off the mark when examined in the harsh light of today's competitive environment. We list some of the frequently heard objections with our comments.

Things move too fast in this industry for us to try to plan where people are going to be two years from now. Besides, it turns out you can't make half of those moves you planned anyway.

How does this same senior executive justify the time spent in developing long-term strategic plans or capital expenditure forecasts, which also are unlikely to prove 100 percent true?

I didn't need a system like that to reach this job. Why does this group of managers need one? Besides we know who the real keepers are anyway.

This comment may be made by an executive who has grown up with the business and to a large part has been responsible for its success. The CEO's legacy should be to leave an organization staffed with managers capable of growing the business well into the future. Yet such an executive, when departing, will more likely leave the organization in a state of disarray. (And ultimate departure is inevitable!)

I'll do the deciding on key personnel decisions (and usually unstated), I don't care to lose or relinquish the decision-making authority, which has been my exclusive domain.

This attitude reflects a genuine fear that may reside in "high–control-oriented" leaders. Their concern is that allowing others' input into executive promotion decisions will erode their power base. But management development systems are not intended to steal power from anyone. Rather, they are intended to improve the quality of decisions made about key people by providing more data and judgment on candidates and on the needs of the jobs to be filled. The CEO who directs a management development system is simply fulfilling a part of his or her legitimate stewardship responsibility and is reflecting true qualities of leadership.

It looks like another paper bureaucracy some consultant dreamed up that will provide an excuse for adding staff and bloating the organization. What's being proposed is part of every executive's job right now. They don't need someone looking over their shoulder, especially corporate staff, to tell them how to do the job!

This may be the response to an overzealous staff person depicting in minute detail every form, timetable, and action that would occur in a fully mature and functioning management development system. If so, our advice to the proponent would be to keep it simple. But more importantly, this response indicates that the senior executive does not take ownership of the management development system or support the need for the effort.

It's just not a priority at this time.

Procrastination is the most difficult obstacle to senior management commitment. The executive professes to agree with the need but never gives it sufficient priority for action. Notwithstanding the influence of a number of constituency groups, most CEOs try to set their own agendas. It is sometimes difficult for a subordinate executive to influence the setting of corporate priorities. In a society so concerned with short-term results, it often takes courage on the part of the CEO to allocate management time and energy to a process for which the payoff may occur during one's successor's term of office.

We may be bought out, so why waste the time?

As we pointed out in chapter 2, the threat of acquisition or merger has been given as an excuse for placing a low priority on the growing of executive talent. The senior executive would argue that the future is too uncertain and that many jobs might be eliminated. Even with fewer jobs, there will still be key jobs to fill after a merger. And a system that has previously ranked individuals according to their relative qualifications can be an invaluable resource. Several years ago, a bank created out of a merger had its professional employees fill out résumés so that management could know of their experience and qualifications. It is regrettable when there are no systems in place that can make such information readily available. Employees often become demoralized when they come to realize that they are virtual unknowns in their own companies.

These are but a half dozen of the many objections that a champion of management development may encounter in working to help create such systems. There are others. But they must not defeat the effort to gain corporate commitment to a process so vital to the long-term success of a corporation.

Gaining corporate commitment does not occur overnight. Exxon has the commitment of its senior management, thanks to almost 50 years of having a management development system. A formal program for executive development was adopted in 1945 by Exxon's predecessor, Standard Oil, two years after a committee had been appointed to study the problem of executive succession and development. In 1946, George Corless, first co-ordinator of executive development for Standard Oil, described the plan as designed for "developing reserves of key personnel comparable to the reserves of physical assets."[6] The comparison of executive resources or "reserves," as Corless called them, with physical assets was no doubt a new concept in the 1940s. Still, today many executives fail to recognize its validity. Even with two years of preparation, a full-time, senior-level co-ordinator, and a charge from the Executive Committee, it took several years for the concept of planned executive development to be adopted and im-plemented by the company's many subsidiaries and organizations. For HR managers and for senior executives who see the implementation of a management development system as moving too slowly, take heart! Under the best of circumstances, it is a slow process.

At Exxon, many senior executives are products of that decades-old system, having spent virtually all of their careers with one company. (The average company service of the top five corporate officers is 35 years!)[7] Exxon executives became committed to management development within their own organizations as lower-level managers. And spending a significant amount of management time in people-related discussion and decision making has always been a normal part of the job.

Don Laidlaw, while corporate director of executive resources for IBM, has described how his senior management has grown up with the system, and as a result, how the CEO sees it as *his* system and *his* responsibility.[8] There is no question as to the commitment of senior management at companies like GE, Exxon, or IBM. But getting the commitment of the senior executive who is not a product of a development system can present a real challenge. Also, it is unlikely that a CEO with a multicorporation career, and who has been recruited from another company, will automatically champion a strong promotion from within doctrine.

However difficult to obtain, the commitment of the CEO and other senior management is required! It must be obtained early in the process to establish a viable system. The necessary corporate commitment is best reflected in a written statement of policy, but it is particularly important that it be exemplified in the day-to-day behaviors and activities of senior executives.

EIGHT INFLUENCE STRATEGIES

It is normal for CEOs to have strong beliefs in their own convictions. After all, a large measure of self-confidence helped greatly in getting them to their current positions. That favorable characteristic also means that the CEO will not be easily moved from a position.

Recognizing that there are variables of personality, trust, corporate culture, experience, and internal politics that will affect the approach taken to sell the CEO and others on succession planning, we offer the following strategies. The "seller" is most likely to be the senior HR officer, although it could be a line manager from an affiliate or division. Regardless of the strategy chosen, the CEO ultimately must believe that introducing a comprehensive management succession planning and executive development system will help the corporation achieve its strategic agenda or help solve pressing problems or issues.

1. **Identify real organizational issues.** Nothing gains "followship" in organizations as quickly as those ideas that promise to solve readily identifiable problems. Gathering hard data regarding people, development needs, staffing attrition, or other organizational problems that a management development system can address will help gain attention at the senior level. Simple projections that reveal when a company can reasonably expect to lose various members of its management team can quickly capture attention. Problems that might indicate the need for a management development system include:
   • Unplanned and unwanted management turnover
   • Attrition of lower-level professionals and managers
   • Absence of readily identifiable replacement candidates
   • Inadequate number of highly talented people in the organization's pipeline
   • Absence of women and minorities in positions in which they can obtain needed developmental experience to prepare them for greater responsibilities
   • Training efforts that appear unfocused or misdirected or where concern exists over the return on the training investment
   • Professional recruiting difficulties

2. **Obtain feedback from employees on attitudes and expectations.** Focus groups and surveys can be used to obtain feedback from employees concerning their thoughts, desires, and concerns regarding career opportunities and development. The feedback can then be presented to senior management. If growth opportunities are indeed limited in the company, the feedback will reflect discontent. Most senior executives are sensitive to the need to maintain their professional employees' morale, and any feedback reflecting discontent will create interest in the need for a management development program.

3. **Develop a pilot program in a division or affiliate.** This strategy is often referred to as "finding a warm nest." A CEO or senior management team may be more comfortable with implementing a pilot program in one unit than with committing the entire corporate energies. As a practical matter, starting with a pilot plan may be desirable even with full corporate commitment. Fully establishing a corporate system often takes two to three years, and piloting in one unit is a practical way to begin a succession planning effort in an organization.

One advantage of using a pilot program to gain corporate commitment is that sponsorship can then come from a line executive rather than from corporate staff. A recommendation coming from a line executive is guaranteed to gain more favorable attention from the senior management.

4. **Benchmark the best practices in successful companies.** Senior executives are naturally interested in the practices of other successful organizations. Benchmarking has become an accepted approach to determining where a company stands relative to its competition. A strategy used by many HR practitioners is to perform an in-depth analysis of other companies and their practices that would be of interest and potential value. Companies within the industry known for having the best practices in HR management, companies *outside* the industry that are similarly known, and direct competitors, regardless of their reputation in the HR area, are all useful to analyze. (Competitors may produce less meaningful data. However, senior management will ask about these companies and it is best to have that homework done.) Benchmarking can often be done with site visits to other companies. A visit can often provide a higher level of understanding than phone calls and documents. Because of the cost, visits may be limited to firms with recognized programs. Yet being able to relate information gained from even a few personal visits will add credibility to the argument for developing a comprehensive system.

5. **Develop a long-range HR plan that emphasizes executive resource needs.** A good long-range HR plan should quantify management resource needs, identify areas of significant shortfall, and highlight the importance of the timely development of management talent. It will also help integrate the "supply" of professional and management resources with the "demand" for management resources. Even if the plan is not used to sell the need for a management development system, it will become an integral part of the management development planning process. Management resource requirements, though based in part on personal judgment, are quantifiable and should relate to availability of talent in the organization.

6. **Draft a pro forma policy statement.** The senior HR officer in any corporation has to identify policy needs that affect management, employees, and the organization. Thus it is well within the area of responsibility of the HR executive to generate a policy relative to succession planning. Most CEOs will not rubber stamp a policy without serious discussion, and a draft policy can stimulate thought

as well as dialogue among senior executives. Of course, if the HR officer is armed with benchmark data, employee feedback, and a plan to support the case for a management development system, there is much greater likelihood that the dialogue will lead to action.

7. **Set a goal.** Include the establishment of a comprehensive, integrated management development system in next year's list of annual objectives. A surprising number of systems in existence today got their start this way. Year after year, an HR executive seeded the idea with senior management until it finally caught on.

8. **Send the CEO a timely article.** The thinking load of senior corporate executives is full and complex. Yet a simple thought or idea expressed by someone outside the company may be the key that opens the door. An article that addresses issues such as different approaches being used in management development, corporate succession, projected shortages of key technical staff, or the costs associated with executive recruitment may be used to identify a problem that cries out for a management development system as part of the solution.

OWNERSHIP

One of the greatest needs we have is to persuade managers at middle and lower levels that they have a responsibility for developing talent and for providing that talent to the corporation.

Walter R. Trosin, Vice President, Merck[9]

The line managers' involvement in developing management talent should easily follow if the commitment and involvement of senior management has been assured. Most successful managers try to respond to the business priorities established by senior management. They are particularly likely to do so with a business priority such as succession planning and management development because they can easily see the potential implications or effects upon them personally.

Assuming that a written policy on management development is clear and well written, it will provide an excellent tool for understanding and for uniform interpretation throughout the company. A document gives managers at all levels a clear signal as to what is expected. In turn, they can uniformly direct their subordinates in implementing the process.

Ideally, line managers become involved because they see the benefit of and believe in developing people to their highest potentials. It has been said that a manager has truly matured when he or she spends more energy on the growth and development of employees than on the furtherance of his or her own career. This kind of manager is usually highly regarded by the employees who, in turn, will produce great results. It is hard to see why managers would be reluctant to involve themselves in people-development activities, regardless of whether or not there is corporate commitment above them.

There are obstacles to involving line managers. Walter R. Mahler and Frank Gaines, Jr., identify as a key obstacle the fact that the executive review process is seen by line managers essentially as an HR activity.[10] Involvement of line managers does not mean turning a project over to someone else. It requires thinking time, getting to know employees, assessing potential, considering individual development plans, and making decisions on promotion and succession—responsibilities that cannot be delegated. Human resources staff or others can help with designing forms, documentation, scheduling of meetings, and program monitoring. But staff cannot undertake the thinking and judgments that are solely the responsibility of line management. These activities, to be effective, require the personal commitment and involvement of the line manager.

Unfortunately, management development accountability does not lend itself as easily to quantifiable objectives and results as do costs, productivity, or sales. Accountability comes through discussion and dialogue. A manager will become fully involved when he or she must meet with a committee of senior management and respond to questions about individuals and their development plans. He or she will not rely on what staff says but will want to respond based on personal knowledge, and that requires involvement.

COMMUNICATING WITH EMPLOYEES

As a middle manager, you're only told what you need to know and sometimes hardly that. . . . The toughest thing about being a middle manager today is that you can't even answer basic questions from your staff. . . . When someone asks you, 'What's my career path?' and you don't have one yourself, what do you say?

Middle manager, Wall Street investment banking firm.[11]

Good employees should know about their companies' management development systems. They are attracted to corporations that provide for the growth and development of employees. Therefore, it would be corporate folly not to let employees and candidates for employment know that there is a system for internal growth and development. In our surveying of classes of MBA students, there is an almost unanimous vote in favor of wanting to work for a company that has such a system.

What is not clear is how much should be communicated and how it should be done. Some companies tend to mask the management development system. Obviously, it is a subject of great interest to employees who will be curious about the details, which they will use to analyze their own careers. Of course, communications will not be taken lightly and it is important that they be well thought out.

There are several ground rules for communication.

1. Policy statements in employee handbooks, recruiting brochures, or other company publications available to all employees should be the vehicle for general communication about the management development system. A policy manual locked in a manager's credenza is not enough. The printed statements should be reformulated as often as appropriate.

2. Communications should be uniform. This alone is a good reason to have and use policy statements that are complete in themselves and will likely remain unchanged.

3. The process itself can be described in the company newsletter and to groups of employees at orientation and training sessions. The description of the management development system should convey that each employee is being given individual attention and that each employee's advancement is a matter of real concern to the organization.

4. It should be made clear that *all* professional and managerial employees are included as part of the system and that the focus is on each employee's achieving his or her highest potential. This does not mean that all employees are to be named on replacement tables, nor should they be.

5. Communications on any one individual's development plans should only be discussed privately. Managers should always exercise caution in talking with employees about the future. There are simply too many variables over which the manager has little control. Many employees have had their expectations dashed when the future does not

measure up to what had been inadvertently communicated to them by supervisors.

6. It need not be a secret that a department committee meets to discuss and review succession plans, individual developmental plans, and a host of related issues. It is prudent, however, that a notice not go up on the bulletin board that such a meeting will be held at 8 A.M. on Tuesday. It is far better that employees think in general terms of the process as continuous, ongoing, and regular.

Above all, common sense will dictate good communications on the total program. Give employees what they need to know to have confidence in the commitment of their management to the process of employee development. Don't burden them with details that may create anxiety or misunderstanding or be difficult to interpret accurately. Common sense will also dictate what a supervisor tells an employee about his or her potential and developmental plans. Be realistic, and wherever possible, strive to make the employee feel good about the future. But do not commit the organization unrealistically or create implied contracts. It is always unfortunate when an organization loses a high-potential employee, especially if the employee leaves because he or she did not understand that there was a bright future ahead in the organization. Likewise, it is devastating to an employee to not receive a promotion that had been indicated, regardless of the circumstances that caused a change in the plans.

CORPORATE COMMITMENT: WHAT HAS CHANGED?

In chapter 1, we talked about the changing environment in which business operates today as compared to a decade ago. We indicated that with a new playing field and new rules, the tried and proven strategies of succession planning and management development are no longer guaranteed to produce winning results. Much of what we have said in this chapter about corporate commitment has been applicable for many years. However, the impact of change does raise several questions.

Is the need for corporate commitment greater today? The answer is yes, for several reasons.

1. Corporate leadership has changed more rapidly due to merger, acquisitions, and severance programs brought about by downsizing. Many organizations are in less certain positions as to the priorities and commitments of their new leadership. The commitment from senior management is not built into the system, and line managers and HR management need clear signals and direction that the management development and succession planning efforts are on the agenda of the senior executive.

2. In more stable times, the momentum of a functioning management development system will carry the effort through changes in senior management. In less stable times, like today in many companies, the system is likely to grind to a halt until a clear signal of corporate commitment is generated.

3. Nurturing and developing potential executives takes on a greater importance as the labor force shrinks and executives are more mobile. More planning will be required to assure the development and readiness of future executives, and corporate commitment will be essential if these resources are to be maintained.

4. A growing number of employees today are more skeptical of corporate leadership, yet they are also concerned about opportunity and their future. Loyalty to the corporation is not a given and must be earned more than ever before. A commitment to management development is important to these employees and that commitment must be visible and clearly communicated.

5. Management decisions are under greater scrutiny by society, government, and the media. Decisions involving executive placement are visible and subject to criticism. Decisions that are based on a sound system for management development will not only be better, but they will be more defensible. Therefore, a commitment to management development is important to external as well as internal relationships.

Is corporate commitment more difficult to obtain? Again, the answer is yes. Let's face it, most corporate management is under great short-term pressures. Some pressure comes from intense competition, now global. Some comes from financial plight brought about by merger or defense against merger. Other pressures come from government regulation or threat of greater regulation. Meeting environmental concerns is becoming a major challenge for many industries. Changing laws and problems involving employees—hiring, health and safety, pension—are requiring some difficult short-term decisions. It's a more challenging time to do business than ever before!

In the face of these short-term needs, it is obviously more difficult to obtain management commitment to the long-term needs of succession planning and management development.

Have the techniques for obtaining corporate commitment changed? The answer is no. The principles and techniques for obtaining management's interest are much the same. The importance of applying these techniques and others that ingenuity may devise, of course, has increased.

CHAPTER CHECK LIST

1. A complete management development system should address the succession plans for key jobs, the developmental plans for individuals, and implementation plans for achieving both.

2. A written policy helps to assure the commitment of senior management and provides a more uniform communications vehicle to employees and future employees. It becomes the framework for establishing the review process and involving management at all levels.

3. Corporate commitment is essential to a viable management development system.

4. Ownership of the system must rest with the line management. Human resources serves as staff support in assisting the line management in carrying out its responsibilities.

5. The policy and process should be communicated to employees and potential employees uniformly, since good people will be attracted to corporations that practice internal management development.

6. Corporate commitment takes on an even greater importance in today's business environment.

Chapter Six

MAKING THE SYSTEM WORK: MUTUAL ROLES AND RESPONSIBILITIES

I f we were to examine the origins of recently implemented management development systems, we might find it difficult to determine exactly where and from whom the effort received its initial impetus. Some systems may have resulted from a seed planted by an HR manager. Others may have resulted from the CEO making the initial determination that something should be done. It is likely, however, that in every case the early process heavily involved both the CEO and the HR manager. It is also likely that HR has contributed an incredible amount of work and energy in getting the program up and running. Fully integrated management development systems just don't fall into place!

We asked Eric Vetter if succession planning is so important, so basic, why isn't everyone doing it? Eric responded: "Well, it's like a lot of other management systems and management practices. It has to be initiated. It has to get sponsorship somewhere, it just doesn't invent itself."[1] And that somewhere (or someone), with encouragement from the CEO, likely is HR.

However, if we were to examine recent succession planning efforts that have failed or fallen short, our belief is that an attribute of most failed efforts would be ownership by HRs. Failure, in our opinion, may have resulted from HR's reluctance to transfer "sponsorship" to the senior management and senior management's reluctance to receive it.

This chapter will define in some detail the mutual roles and responsibilities of the CEO, HR management, line management, the board of directors, and employees in making a management development system work.

THE CEO

Jack Welch, chairman and CEO of General Electric, was asked, "What is the one most important thing you do?" He replied, "The people process." He then went on to discuss the importance of his using his time in the selection of candidates for key positions and in other activities having to do with the development of people in the organization.[2] John B. McCoy, chairman of Banc One Corporation, has expressed similar sentiments: "My role is chief personnel officer. If I get the right people in the right jobs, that's all I have to do."[3]

Of course, the CEO position is far more complex than just following the development of people and then leaving the rest up to them. A job description for many CEOs could, in addition to people development, include such duties as being a: cheerleader and motivator, corporate spokesperson, strategic planner, and a tough decision-maker. These activities are usually visible and are more likely to be reflected in the media than "people development" activity. But we believe, that in all cases, people development should be of the highest priority.

In chapter 5, we pointed out the need for the involvement and commitment from the CEO if a management development system is to be effective. We also gave some strategies for HR staff to use in gaining the commitment of the CEO and senior management. As to the role of the CEO we would like to offer several recommendations:

1. The CEO should be a role model for other executives in giving visible attention to the management development process.

2. The CEO should initiate the development of, participate in, and personally "sign off" on a management development *policy*, which includes a commitment to promotion from within to the extent possible.

3. The CEO should hold subordinate managers accountable for the development of people.

4. The CEO should be the force behind and actively participate in regular reviews of succession and management development plans for all significant organizational components and the decisions to be made on key staffing.

There is little question that when the CEO demonstrates a commitment to management development and the importance of devoting time and energy to the process, managers at all levels will respond with a greater commitment of their own.

Much has been written on the role of the CEO and styles of leadership. "Does the CEO Really Matter?" was the title of a *Fortune* magazine article by Patricia Sellers. She wrote of the role of the CEO that "He—or she—must be able to handle three critical jobs exceptionally well: Set the corporate strategy, get the employees aligned behind it, and develop a successor."[4] We agree. However, developing a successor is more than just making a decision on one, or even several candidates. To us it is taking responsibility for a system that will develop people at all levels in the organization.

Sellers used the example of PepsiCo. She pointed out that Wayne Calloway, CEO, spends about half his time on personnel issues and meets with hundreds of middle managers each year to review their progress.[5] So the role of the CEO as it applies to management development is quite simple. It is to place the highest priority on "people," as GE's Jack Welch says, and to expect that all managers will embrace that same priority.

HUMAN RESOURCE MANAGEMENT

In our 1991 survey of practices in management development and succession planning, we asked respondents to assess the level of success on 17 management development issues. The issue reflecting the highest score was:

> "Knowledgeable, credible and capable human resources staff who support the management development and succession planning system."

Given that the survey was mailed to HR executives, we admit that some bias may be reflected in the responses. However, the survey results are consistent with the opinion generally held today on the overall quality and professionalism of HR staff.

It is logical that staff responsibility for management development falls with HR, but there are exceptions. For many years in Exxon Corporation, the staff manager for executive development reported to the corporate secretary and remained totally outside of HR (then called Employee Relations). There was a rationale for keeping executive development separate. It helped preserve the confidentiality of information and probably gave line managers a greater degree of "ownership." However, in our opinion, it is more appropriate for HR to have full staff responsibility for the management development system. This is particularly true today in view of the high level of expertise, credibility, and knowledge that exists in most HR organizations.

For a large organization with thousands of employees, the staff role for executive development may require one manager-level employee and supporting administrative personnel. There are some clear advantages to giving longer tenure to the executive development manager (although the same could be said for many key management positions.) It is difficult for senior management to place full trust in a manager handling such sensitive information if it is felt that he or she will soon be moving out into other corporate assignments. Also, earning credibility with line management is important to the success of an executive development manager, and that takes time. A large majority of the HR executives responding to our survey indicated that the position for administering the management development system in their organization was not itself used for management development.

Sometimes staff responsibility for management development is placed solely with the HR vice president or manager; if this happens, the management development function becomes a key part of that job description. Walter R. Trosin, vice president for human resources at Merck, described his responsibility:

> On an overall corporate basis it is my personal responsibility to orchestrate, [to] provide for the design and implementation of the succession planning system for Merck executives. That means in addition to working with the line people and personnel people throughout the corporation and affecting a good design that I arrange for the timing and implementation and the scheduling of the various sessions, take notes, and act as catalyst at the corporate sessions.[6]

The key words here are "orchestrate" and "catalyst." The words do not imply ownership or direction. Rather they describe an action-oriented staff role.

Steve McMahon described the role of HR in management development when he was HR vice president at Fireman's Fund Insurance:

> To me, a staff group like human resources is really a facilitator. They *help* make things happen. They don't make things happen. There's a real difference. The actual decision-making, the activity, the execution of whatever outcome, comes from the line management. They have to own it. They have to commit to it. I see Human Resources as playing a staff role in providing a process, helping work out the details—but not making the decision, not being the one in charge.[7]

The role of the executive development staff (presumably in the HR department and possibly even the senior HR executive) consists of several key responsibilities:

Developing Policy

The CEO must determine the key issues in a management development policy. However, HR staff can plant the seed by drafting of policy and engaging in dialogue with senior executives. Getting a review of policy on the CEO's agenda is not always easy, particularly if the CEO is not receptive. And it may take some courage to broach the subject. But if it results in persuading the CEO of the importance of taking a stand on management development, it will be worth the risk.

Designing, Scheduling, and Coordinating the Review Process

The mechanics of the review process are clearly HR's responsibility—from early design to full implementation. Although instructions should come out over the signature of a senior line executive, the writing of the instructions and the many phone calls required to determine a final review schedule normally will be performed by HR staff.

Advising Senior Management

"It's lonely at the top" is an expression with particular meaning as applied to executive succession and development. The CEO needs someone in whom to confide and with whom to discuss people at the highest levels. The HR executive who develops that level of confidential relationship will be able to significantly impact the management development process. However, it is a relationship and trust that must be earned. Reginald Jones, former chairman of GE, commented that in his 10 years as chairman, he probably had more private and one-on-one meetings with Ted LeVino, the staff executive in charge of GE's executive resources program than with any other single individual.[8] That same relationship can exist with other members of senior management. It is probably common for an HR executive responsible for management development to be called into the office of a senior line executive to discuss succession within a particular department or plans for a specific high-potential individual. The trust level must be such that the parties can engage in those very private conversations.

Advising Line Management

The person responsible for management development also can be invaluable to line managers throughout the organization. But as with senior management, trust must be earned through the careful handling of confidential information. Since the development of a confidential relationship takes time, the longer tenure of the HR executive is most desirable.

The HR executive must be available to line managers. It would be a serious mistake to develop a close relationship with senior corporate executives and not be equally as available to lower-level managers in the organization. Line managers also need someone to talk to about sensitive matters, and they need someone to counsel them on their presentations in the management development review process. They also need help in the coordination of recommendations on interfunctional moves. Some of the real rewards for the HR executive come from being able to help line managers throughout the organization with their roles in the management development process. The successful HR executive will function as staff to the entire corporate organization, not just to the senior management. It is a role that can be both extremely challenging and enormously fulfilling.

Participating in Reviews

There is no one pattern for how the HR executive must participate in management development and succession planning reviews. It will depend on the CEO's wishes and the HR executive's knowledge and experience. In short, participating should be on a value added basis.

Typically, the HR executive will serve as secretary to the proceedings, making it unnecessary to bring in secretarial staff, and thus encouraging candid discussion. Only the decisions need recording, so there is no need to transcribe conversation verbatim. In fact, it would be counterproductive.

Should the HR executive freely express judgments about people and plans during the review? Although it depends on the relationship between the HR executive and the senior management, the answer is probably no unless the CEO requests them. It should be clear that the decisions are being made by the senior management, not by HR. The most effective way for the HR executive to give input on decisions is through one-on-one discussions that take place as the plans are being developed by the line managers, and this requires having high credibility with those managers.

Helping others (senior and line management) achieve the desired results from the management development system best describes HR's role. Individual relationships will be key to how well that help is accepted.

Maintaining the Data

It is the clear responsibility of the HR executive to be the keeper of succession and individual plan data. It is our belief that the documentation should be of decisions and plans, not of discussion and opinions.

Monitoring the Development Process

Senior management should look to HR to track the management development process and monitor results. It will expect HR to identify weaknesses and problem areas calling for management attention. HR should be proactive in the analysis of data and trends. This may include special reports on women and minorities, supply and demand for specific skills and talents, and the impact of potential changes in size and scope of the business. Above all, it is HR that will develop the "gut feel" that the system is, or is not, working to provide the desired results of competent, ready managers for future staffing.

Figure 6-1 depicts the ideal position of HR in the management development system. In this scheme, HR is the focal point in the organization. It has direct accountability only to the CEO but provides advice and counsel to senior corporate management and lower-level line managers. It provides advice to the directors only on call (we suspect, unfortunately, that does not occur often in most corporations). HR's accountability to the CEO is primarily for the mechanics of the system, maintaining data, and monitoring performance by the line organization.

LINE MANAGEMENT

The line organization must be an extension of the CEO in directing and implementing a system for management development. Of course, each organization presents a different set of circumstances. For example, some

Figure 6-1
Role of Human Resources in the Managment Development System

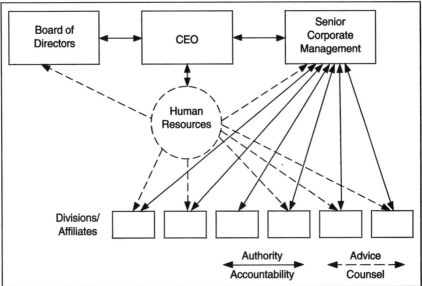

organizations are very decentralized with each division head or subsidiary president having almost complete autonomy. In these organizations, it will take a strong CEO to "centralize" management development if centralization in any form is contrary to the corporate culture and organization philosophy.

One decentralization technique is for the CEO and senior corporate management to retain control over three resource allocation mechanisms—staffing levels, compensation systems, and capital budgets—while leaving the subordinates responsible for obtaining results. This is not always satisfactory to some unit heads, but it works. Division managers feel that they are making their own decisions, even though their hands are somewhat tied in three very important areas. However, the division managers are accorded great respect because they make recommendations in the three areas not under their control, and their recommendations are often acceptable. The control held over staffing (and to some degree the compensation system) provides the opportunity for dialogue between the CEO and the division manager and the opportunity to discuss people, their compensation, and development.

A truly autonomous division or subsidiary head should follow the recommendations shown for the CEO above—be a role model, sign off on
policy, hold subordinates accountable for development, and participate in
reviews and dialogue. Line managers are in the chain of the management
development process, and the chain will only be as good as its weakest link.

BOARD OF DIRECTORS

In trying to define the role of corporate directors in the process of management development, we can only make general recommendations, since
boards operate in many different ways. Some directors exert a great deal
of control over staffing, particularly at the senior levels. Other directors
have, at best, only a passive interest and leave the decision making to the
corporate executives. In some corporations, directors are major shareholders
while in others they may hold only token shares.

Thomas R. Horton, former chairman of the American Management
Association, has described three anomalies about corporate boards. First,
they are populated by directors who are hand-selected by the chief executives, to whom they are therefore indebted. Second, outside directors know
something, but not necessarily very much, about the specific business because conflict-of-interest considerations bar directors from their own industries. Third, this lack of industry-specific knowledge is often overcome
by the inclusion of inside directors whose very presence may at times inhibit
frank discussion by the directors.[9]

It appears that corporate boards are exerting more control today than
in the past. A feature article in the *Wall Street Journal* in the summer of
1991 was headlined "Tense Times: More Chief Executives Are Being
Forced Out By Tougher Boards."[10] Examples of fallen CEOs appear frequently in the news, and those former CEOs have, no doubt, gained firsthand experience concerning the power of the board of directors.

Still, most boards of major corporations in fact exert relatively little control
over the long- and short-term conduct of the business. To illustrate, consider
a large, publicly held corporation. There are 12 outside and three employee
directors. Of the 12 outside directors, five are CEOs of major corporations,
two are recently retired CEOs, two are well-known consultants, one is a
banker, one is a university president, and one is a prominent lawyer. Each
of the outside directors is on the board of at least one other publicly held

corporation. None owns as much as a fraction of one percent of the total shares, and most were not shareholders before being elected to the board.

In this hypothetical corporation, outside directors chair, among others, three board committees: Audit, Compensation, and Nominating. The board meets 12 times during the year, and board committees meet two to three times per year. The pay is token by executive pay standards—about $50,000 for a committee chair who attends most meetings. The stated mission of the board is to establish broad corporate policies and to oversee the overall performance of the corporation.

An analysis of our board profile would lead to four observations:

1. All outside directors (except possibly the retired CEOs) have full-time, high-profile responsibilities elsewhere and are not likely to have the time or inclination to follow the activities of the corporation or to study and fully learn the operations and business.

2. Prestige is the primary motivator in accepting a directorship, although most directors and the corporations for whom they work will rationalize some business benefit. "Name recognition" would appear to influence the selection of many directors.

3. It is likely that directors will rely on corporate staff for any information on HR development.

4. Outside directors will want to fulfill their responsibilities with the expenditure of as little time and energy as possible.

If this is a typical profile for a large corporation board, then how does this board contribute to the process of management development and succession planning?

The answer: In most cases it doesn't.

But is that the right answer? We say, emphatically, no! If the board takes seriously its responsibility for establishing broad corporate policy, then it should direct attention to the policy for succession planning and management development. In fact, that should be a top priority in assuring the corporation's long-range health. It is possible that a director, based on his or her own corporate experience, may ask some questions about the management development policy and may be given some written information. But the director is likely to feel that he or she has fulfilled the director responsibility just by raising the questions.

So again, do we conclude that the board has no role in management development? Not at all. What we do conclude is that it is unrealistic to expect that the board members will have the time, motivation, or understanding to become more than minimally involved with management development. (Granted, there are exceptions to this conclusion.)

Corporate boards do have responsibility for determining the CEO's successors as well as the authority to discharge the CEO. That fact became painfully apparent to Rod Canion, cofounder and CEO of Compaq Computer in October 1991. One Wednesday, Canion announced that Compaq would lay off about 1,400 workers, or 12 percent of the workforce, in what he described as "one of the most difficult decisions I have ever had to make."[11] On Thursday, the corporate board, in a 14-hour meeting, decided that Canion was to be the first to go.[12] On Friday, the business world and employees learned that Canion, the individual who had been widely acclaimed for his role in building Compaq into a multibillion dollar success story in just a few years, had actually been replaced. Ironically, on Saturday, *Business Week* hit the street with an article on Compaq with liberal quotes from Rod Canion and his strategies for the future.[13] (In the Compaq case, influential directors were also major investors and thus more motivated to take action than would have been directors of the corporation in our example.)

Those "four days in October" illustrate that a board of directors' greatest potential impact lies with the "stick" it holds over the CEO. With that in mind, we offer several recommendations to boards of directors regarding management development.

1. Delegate to the appropriate committee (either Nominating or possibly Management Development and Compensation) responsibility for oversight of the management development system.

2. Request and carefully review the corporate policy on management development. If none exists, insist that one be developed.

3. Request the succession proposal for the CEO and other senior-level positions from corporate management. Meet with the CEO to question and understand the recommendations.

4. Require identification of internal candidates to reduce or eliminate outside hires. If management pleads that no such candidates are qualified, ask them to pursue inside candidates who are most nearly qualified and discuss what can be done to qualify them.

5. In line with the oversight responsibility of the board, require that an audit of the complete management development process be conducted by in-house staff. If management feels incapable of dedicating staff time, an outside consultant can be used. The focus of the audit

should be on the development of individual employees. The audit should address the broad areas of management commitment and involvement, review procedures, stewardship and accountability, bench strength, potential assessment, and employee development. It should address substantive issues more than just tables and charts.

The process involves having the directors ask tough questions. The answers themselves are not as important as the message to management that "it had better get with the program." Our simple premise in management development is that when managers are forced to dedicate thinking energy to HR planning and to the assessment of individuals, they will use good judgment. Directors can force that expenditure of thinking energy by some tough questions on internal management development. Hopefully, the effort will leverage an even greater expenditure of that thinking energy by managers at lower levels.

These recommendations are most applicable to larger corporations. In smaller corporations, the role of the directors may be different, particularly in those corporations in which the directors have a significant financial stake. The differences come from the fact that directors of smaller corporations will be more interested in both the short-term and long-term success of the business, willing to invest a greater amount of time, and have a more intimate knowledge of the business and its employees. For these directors, we suggest taking an even greater role in assuring that a viable management development system is functioning.

EMPLOYEES

In our opinion, the greatest impact of our changing business environment on the management development process has to do with the change in employee attitudes and values. Employees are key to the process—they are the reason for the process—and as they change, so must the system.

Judith M. Bardwick writes about the changing employment contract in *Danger in the Comfort Zone: From Boardroom to Mailroom—How to Break the Entitlement Habit That's Killing American Business:*

> The contract of understanding and obligation between employers and employees has changed. Most of our organizations, but especially those that enjoyed decades of *entitlement*, maintained a powerful and implicit contract with their employees. In exchange for unswerving loyalty and a level of commitment that

entailed putting the company before family or self, you had a position for life. The company invested in you and took care of you . . .[14]

In that entitlement age referred to by Bardwick, the role of the employee was to accept that the company was looking out for his or her development and that the choice of the next assignment would be in the best interest of the employee as well as the company.

From a management development perspective, this was an excellent arrangement. Plans could be made by the company and could be kept secret. And the company could expect that the employee would loyally accept any assignment chosen by the company. It was not all bad from the employee perspective either. He or she could know that doing a good job was the key to success, and that it was not necessary to worry about or try and select the next assignment. It was not necessary to keep updating a résumé. It was an employer–employee relationship of mutual trust.

But today we are faced with a "trust gap," as Thomas R. Horton and Peter C. Reid refer to it.[15] Mutual trust no longer exists in most situations. Of necessity, the employee must be involved in the process of determining his or her future career, and he or she has some responsibility for assessing skills and talents as well as for determining ultimate career objectives. The difficulty comes from the variables involved. The company cannot commit to future opportunities (in fact, the company may not know the future shape of the organization). And the employee cannot, or likely will not, commit to a future career without knowing the alternatives. So any discussion of careers will be replete with vague and qualified statements. An abbreviated dialogue between a manager and employee in career counseling might go like this:

Manager: We think you have shown real potential to move into marketing and advance through marketing management. Would you be interested in moving out as a sales district manager if the opportunity were available?

Employee: Suppose I stay in manufacturing, what will my next assignment be?

Manager: That is hard to forecast, since we see no immediate advancement opportunities. But, frankly, the marketing route looks like the best one for you. How do you feel about that?

Employee: Where would I be assigned if I agreed?

Manager: That would be impossible to say at this time. It could be anywhere in the United States based on the available opportunity.

Employee: Suppose I decide I don't like marketing, could I get back into manufacturing?

The point of this is that the savvy employee is not likely to commit to a future career, or even fully indicate his or her desires, until all options are known. And it is impossible for the company to know what those options will be.

Still in this plethora of unknowns, we consider that today the employee has a clear role in the management of his or her own career. We refer to it as a "shared responsibility," by the employer and the employee, and we will enlarge on this subject in chapter 10.

CHAPTER CHECK LIST

1. Efforts to fix responsibility for management development can detract from the substance of the program itself. Yet each part of the organization does have some responsibility for management development. The greatest part of the responsibility is to contribute to the team effort to identify and develop management talent for the entire organization.

2. The CEO's commitment is the linchpin, so the primary role of the CEO is to demonstrate that commitment.

3. HR staff must provide the support, energy, intelligence, and mechanics and see to it that the management development machinery is oiled and well maintained. The staff executive offers an additional role to the CEO and lower levels of line management, as the confidant in very sensitive and private discussions about people.

4. Line management must maintain ownership of the management development system and provide judgment in the planning for individual development.

5. The board has a role only if it wants to. Historically it has been unrealistic, in most cases, to expect much from the board on management development. This is not as it should be, and perhaps it will change as more active voices make known their views regarding involvement and accountability at the board level.

6. Employees, the most often overlooked, are also participants and have a shared responsibility for their career development. Not only should they be communicated with, but they should be listened to not only on their personal desires but on the application of the entire management development system to them.

7. Above all, the roles of various parts of the organization are not set in concrete. They will vary based on corporate governance, individual personalities, corporate culture, and business dynamics. The key is to establish those roles in a manner that will optimize those variables and result in a process that is contributed to by the entire corporate team.

Chapter Seven

REVIEW AND STEWARDSHIP

The purpose of the review by the Corporate Management Committee is for senior executives to report on their people, on the development process in place. It is an inspection process to make sure that each unit of the organization has a system in place to identify people for the IBM corporation.

Don Laidlaw, Corporate Director, Executive Resources IBM[1]

THE REVIEW PROCESS

Most succession planning and management development practitioners would identify the senior-level review as the heart of a functioning management development system. The review is the mechanism by which senior management demonstrates its commitment to the system, gains information on the judgments about key employees, develops succession plans, and audits the functioning of the management development system within the various parts of the corporation.

In our opinion, there is no one format for a senior-level management development review. The review will reflect the organizational culture, the history of the process within the corporation, senior management's level of commitment, and the CEO's management style.

Of the HR executives we surveyed, 70 percent said that management development and succession planning reviews were required at least annually. The majority of respondents also said that at their companies, the standing corporate review committee consisted of from four to eight members and met at least twice a year.

We asked Eric Vetter what the senior management group can learn from the succession planning review. He replied:

I think it tells us a number of things. It tells us what we have in the organization in the way of talent. It tells us how they are doing and how they might be doing in the future. It tells us who might be able to fill a position if it becomes vacant now or in six months. And it tells us about our management exposures. It identifies positions with no back-up where we might have to go outside or stretch to fill, and action steps needed to fill the gap.[2]

Then Vetter added, "It tells us a tremendous amount about how our managers, who are involved in a succession planning process, operate in their organization."

We think Vetter's last point is extremely important. It portrays the senior-level review as an integration of business operations with the development of managers and executives. The level, intensity, and depth of thinking inherent in the dialogue makes the review an extremely valuable business process.

We also asked Vetter to name some of the outcomes of a typical management succession planning review, whether at the senior or lower corporate levels. His response:

There are three kinds of outcomes that take place during the review process. (1) We're going to come to certain agreements. We will agree on appraisals, assessments, back-up candidates and the kind of things that ought to be done. (2) We will determine the need for more information. And (3) we will identify action steps to correct deficiencies or problems.[3]

Of course, whether decisions are made during the review will be the CEO's call. Sometimes the dialogue can be more thought-provoking and beneficial if an immediate decision isn't required. In some organizations, the presenting manager may already have decision-making authority so he or she is looking more for guidance and direction than approval. "Coming to agreement" is a good concept. It implies a meeting of the minds between senior management and line managers. It can apply to very specific staffing decisions or to broad direction.

To better describe how the review process fits into the management development system, we offer the examples of IBM and Weyerhaeuser.

In 1967, IBM launched an executive resources program aimed at developing or ensuring the development of a reservoir of executive level talent, primarily through on-the-job development. The program had a high level of management focus and involvement at all managerial levels. The explicitly stated mission of the program is: "To assure that the Corporation has sufficient qualified individuals to staff its executive positions worldwide in a timely fashion."

The mission at IBM is accomplished by meeting the following goals:

1. the identification of replacement candidates for all key executive positions in sufficient number and with at least one candidate capable of assuming the job at the time the replacement planning is done, thus providing a choice at the time the position comes open (additionally, there is a focus on future jobs for the current incumbent);
2. career planning and development for individuals in the program, assuring logical opportunities for them to strengthen management's perception of their capabilities for the "close-in" on the positions forecast for them; and
3. developmental exposures, both on and off-the-job (educational courses), to further hone the skills of the participating individuals.

These goals are accomplished through line management, which is instrumental in selecting the participants, structuring the appropriate growth experiences, and ensuring the development of those in the program. The executive resources staff, both corporate and divisional, supports line management and helps management in selecting appropriate courses of action.

To assure that these goals are met by every IBM organization, affiliate and subsidiary, the Corporate Management Committee (CMC)—the senior-most executive review and decision-making body of IBM—provides annual oversight. The CMC conducts an executive resources review with each division, subsidiary, or corporate staff head at least once each year or as otherwise requested. The intent of these reviews is to assess the overall planning for executive resources for that unit by exchanging views on key executives' effectiveness, their potential, and their development plans. Also discussed are the unit's high-potential individuals and replacement candidates for key positions.

The review dates are established by the secretary of the CMC, the unit head, and the director of executive resources at corporate headquarters. The unit head (division president, subsidiary president, or corporate staff head) and the director of executive resources jointly determine the material to be covered in the review. The unit head conducts the review with IBM's chairman; president; senior VP, Operations & Services Staff; senior VP, General Business Group; senior VP, Data Processing Complex; senior VP or group executive for the unit; senior line executive or corporate staff head for the unit; and the director of executive resources.

Weyerhaeuser also began in the late 1970s to make provisions for executive continuity. Following a series of internal meetings at which management succession and executive development were the primary topics of discussion, CEO George Weyerhaeuser approved this brief but significant statement of policy:

- The development of a sufficient number of quality replacements is a responsibility of each manager and is equally as important as efficiency, costs, and productivity.
- Systematic and organized efforts must be made to ensure that the development of tomorrow's key managers is not left to chance.
- Therefore, once each year senior management will conduct a thorough review of the management capability in all operating units, businesses, and departments.

Similar to IBM, oversight responsibility was established at the senior management level to carry out the annual review of management capability. Specifically, Weyerhaeuser management wanted to make sure the following objectives were achieved:

- That organization structures and key assignments were thought through and are sound.
- That accurate performance assessments were made so that choices about the development and placement of individuals in the organization would be based on demonstrated ability, the individual's career objectives, and the organization's need.
- That management replacement needs were identified on a regular basis and were part of the company's business plans, and that the best replacement candidates that the company had to offer were identified and developed to support the business plans.
- That employees with outstanding potential were sought out early in their careers and provided with the development and advancement necessary to realize their ultimate potentials.

As part of its review process, Weyerhaeuser established questions to be answered by each vice president, general manager, or department head annually:

1. Organization
   - What changes, if any, do you anticipate making in the next three years in positions reporting directly to you?
   - What changes, if any, for positions two levels below you?

2. Replacement for Your Position
   - Who are the best candidates to qualify for your position?
   - What are the development needs of these candidates to better prepare them to fill your position?
   - What specific development plans do you propose for each candidate?

3. Evaluation of Direct Reports
   - What are the present performance levels and performance improvement needs of your direct reports?
   - What are the career plans and development needs of your direct reports?
   - Your view?
   - Their view?

4. Replacement for Your Direct Reports
   - What is the nature and timing of moves, if any, for individuals in the positions reporting to you?
   - Who do you see as replacement candidates for your direct reports?
   - What are their development plans to qualify them more fully as replacement candidates?

5. High Potentials
   - Who are the high-potential people in your organization?
   - What is the nature and timing of specific developmental actions for these people?

6. Females/Minorities
   - Who are the females and minorities in your organization who have shown capability for advancement?
   - What is the nature and timing of specific developmental actions for these people?

7. Other HR Issues
   - What are the significant constraints/barriers or opportunities to productive and sound HR management in your organization?

8. Action Planning
   - Review results accomplished in the last 12 months.
   - Summarize actions that you plan to take in the next 12 months.

Similar review processes have been adopted by many organizations, large and small, over the past two decades. The process employed by corporations such as General Electric or Exxon operate with greater ease because the tradition has been established over a long period.

You don't build a building from the top down. Likewise, management development does not start from the top, and it will likely fail if it is not built on a solid foundation. Although the commitment must come from the top, the management development review system itself should start at the bottom and roll up to the senior level. Those employees who are now being discussed in a senior-level review were identified and started on their journey to senior management many years earlier.

The Continuous Cycle

Given the almost half century that Exxon's management development system has existed, its review process may be atypical. But it illustrates that a management development system can (and should) operate on a continuous cycle. The review system used by Exxon USA (the domestic operating arm of Exxon Corporation) flows on a continuous annual cycle, shown in Figure 7-1. The schedule may be altered from time to time, but the pattern is always the same. In the example detailed below, the process begins in February with senior management's development of the annual review program, and the cycle is completed in January of the next year with the final corporate review.

Step 1. *February*	• Executive development staff manager develops the review instructions and schedule for final approval by senior management. • Senior management meets to agree on instructions and any particular emphasis it wants to have placed during the reviews (for example, special discussion on development of minorities, professional recruiting, or steps being taken to retain professionals). • Instructions and schedule sent to managers of departments and subsidiaries over CEO's signature.
Step 2. *March*	• Departments set schedule for lower-level reviews and send instructions to next level of units (divisions, refineries, headquarters sections, etc.). • Divisions send instructions to districts.
Step 3. *April*	• Districts meet to develop high-potential lists and individual developmental plans.

> • Division management holds review with each district manager and reaches agreement on lists and developmental plans and lower-level succession plans.

Step 4.
May
> • Department management holds review with division managers to reach agreement on high-potential lists and developmental plans. Review usually involves all division managers and key department managers, including department HR manager. Review can last from one to two days, enabling each division manager to fully discuss individuals and their developmental plans.

Step 5.
June
July
August
> • Senior management holds review for each department and subsidiary. Only department manager or subsidiary president and executive development staff manager attend. Reviews for each large department or subsidiary scheduled for half a day and for small departments, two hours.

Step 6.
September
October
> • Senior management will meet with executive development staff manager to discuss replacement tables for senior-level positions and development plans for senior-level executives.

Step 7.
November
December
January
> • Executive development staff manager works with CEO to develop overall replacement tables for key positions, including senior management, and developmental plans for senior executives.
> • CEO holds review with senior management to discuss replacement plans and developmental plans for higher-level positions and executives. Similar reviews held for other worldwide operations.
> • CEO reports to senior management on corporate review and decisions.

Not everyone in the Exxon organization will perceive the review process as a closed annual cycle. At lower levels it will be perceived as one of several important projects to be completed during the year. There will be the capital budget reviews, the expense forecasts, the update of the expense forecasts, the salary budget, performance appraisals—all at different times

FIGURE 7-1
Continuous Review System

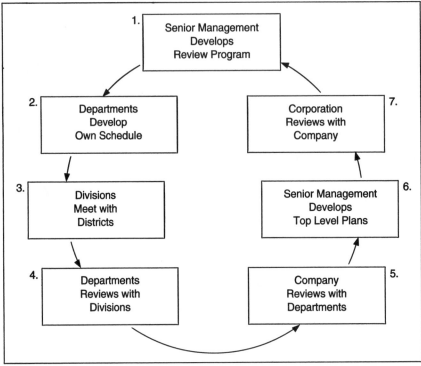

of the year. But when spring comes, the division manager is likely to say, "It's management development time again!"

Also, it would be misleading to imply that reviews are as complete as indicated at lower levels in every department. Some managers may take shortcuts. However, the importance of the review process, which has been demonstrated by the senior management, assures that a high level of involvement will take place, even by the lowest level of line managers.

The review process requires a significant commitment to meeting time, not always a popular thing with busy managers, yet there is no substitute for the face-to-face discussions about people. In our opinion, if you could prioritize the value of the use of time by managers, the time spent in meetings on management development would be at the top of the list.

THE SENIOR-LEVEL REVIEW

Today's successful leaders will work diligently to engage others in their cause. Oddly enough, the best way, by far, to engage others is by listening—serious listening—to them.

Tom Peters, *Thriving on Chaos*[4]

The senior-level review committee at Exxon USA consists of the same five top executives as does the management committee. When handling matters of executive development and compensation, it calls itself the Compensation and Executive Development (C&ED) or COED Committee, with the executive development staff manager providing staff support. The five-person committee provides the linkage or integration with the strategic business planning discussed in chapter 3. Although the CEO may carry the deciding vote, most CEOs will have grown up under committee management and will tend to let the committee decision-making process work.

For each management development review at Exxon, books are prepared for the committee members including department succession plans and plans for high-potential employees. For easy reference, the books also include organization charts and personal history forms on the people included in the plans.

The senior-level review, at which the department manager presents to the C&ED Committee, performs several useful purposes:

1. **Departmental stewardship of the management development system**
   It is the opportunity for senior management to satisfy itself that the department is doing a satisfactory job in its identification of potential and in the implementation of development plans. This is what Don Laidlaw of IBM refers to as the inspection process.

2. **Opportunity for open and candid discussion about key employees, changes in their potential, and their development plans**
   Good decisions on staffing do not come out of a textbook. Rather they are the product of thoughtful discussion and debate. The senior-level review provides opportunity for that debate on key people.

3. **Approval, often with changes made during the review, of the department's succession and development plans**

4. **Forum for the discussion of organizational changes that may
   impact management development without the burden of having to make a final decision on organization** (organization decisions will be handled in a separate review)

The ambience of the review session is important. The environment
should be conducive to a constructive and productive dialogue. A relaxed
atmosphere with a minimum of structured presentation or discussion seems
to produce the best results. It encourages thoughtful debate, which will
produce the sound judgments. The opinions of the presenter are of great
importance to senior management, who should listen and question with
great interest.

At Exxon, decisions on job appointments are usually deferred until closer
to when the job change will occur. Of course, if the move was included
in the management development plans discussed in the review, it is usually
approved in short order when the time to act comes. But a second meeting
provides an opportunity for more dialogue. Clearly, at Exxon, decisions on
people and filling key jobs are not made lightly or without ample discussion!

If you were to sit in on an Exxon review you probably would leave with
a very warm feeling about the management and their commitment to the
development of their employees. You would have witnessed several hours
of candid but substantive discussion, teamwork between senior management
and the department manager, mutual respect, and a visionary commitment.

Steve McMahon says of the senior-level reviews he participated in at
Fireman's Fund, "The discussion was the key. We were interested in having
managers talk about people in a substantive way; what they felt were the
strengths and weaknesses, who was ready now and what needed to happen
for someone to be ready for a job."[5]

Walter Trosin also places great value in the discussion. He says, "Only
three or four people attend the review at Merck. The reason for limiting
attendance is that the degree of honesty, the degree of candor, the level
of quality of the discussion, and dialogue increase with the smaller number
of people in the room. We want dialogue more than presentation."[6]

For the Company Getting a Late Start

We offer several suggestions for firms desiring a disciplined, integrated
management development review process but that do not have the benefit
of years of experience and acceptance. (More on this appears in chapter
13.)

1. Establish a management development policy. Things can begin to happen only after that initial first step.

2. If a management committee or executive committee does not already exist, form a committee of senior management to take responsibility for management development.

3. Be patient. The benefits of the review process may take several years to develop. Don't expect instant success.

4. Set a long-range plan with attainable steps each year. Steps could include: assigning responsibility for staff support for the management development system, widely disseminating the management development policy, and scheduling a series of reviews by senior management with department managers. Items of business for reviews could include:
   - Identification and discussion of 15 highest potential employees with minimum of 5 years service
   - Recommended development plans for those employees
   - Succession plans for top 15 department positions
   - Discussion of overall developmental needs for the department
   - Developing a succession plan for top 25 corporate positions, following the first round of department reviews
   - Implementing interfunctional moves for three high-potential employees
   - Providing staff assistance to each department on establishing a review process at lower levels (larger operating departments would be given first priority)
   - Requesting that each department develop a secondary list of the next 15 high-potential employees with 5 or more years of service and a list of high-potential employees with less than 5 years of service (this will help move the process down lower in the organization)
   - Providing management training in potential assessment

5. Get started—do it, try it, fix it! Work on the concept of continuous improvement versus achieving perfection.

STEWARDSHIP

The department manager's stewardship or accountability for the management development program is necessarily evaluated in the senior-level review. However, keeping score on the percentage of goals met is a little unfair, since only the senior management may have the authority to implement plans, and projections about specific jobs are extremely difficult if not impossible to make. Stewardship will be measured on the successful development of candidates and on the availability of candidates to fill positions. It is on this development of candidates that senior management will be judging the line managers. The manager who "wings" the review, without a solid development program to describe, will be easily exposed.

We asked Dick Holmberg, manager of compensation and management development for Exxon USA, how rapid organizational change was influencing the senior-level reviews at Exxon. Dick pointed out that the reviews have continued to follow the traditional format, but the focus of the discussion is on the development of people and getting them ready to take on more responsibility, rather than on the succession tables. He said that the dialogue between committee members and department heads primarily involves the capabilities of the people, the development needs for the organization, and understanding of the resource base.

Talking to Holmberg left us with the impression that Exxon was not diminishing the attention traditionally given to management development. Rather, as the business continues to change in unprecedented ways, senior executives are using the management development system, including the review process, to assure the development of the executive resources required to meet the anticipated business needs. Dick closed our interview with this bit of wisdom: "In chaotic times, you don't abandon the process!"[7]

Throughout this book, we have stated our belief that the focus in management development should be on the people, not on the positions. It is interesting that Exxon has placed its focus, in both the review process and stewardship, on the development of the people for a more practical reason: the need to meet the demands of a rapidly changing organization.

Ultimately, the quality of stewardship rests on the success or failure of the people who have been identified and developed, and these outcomes may take years to unfold. Therefore, it is important that senior management use the review and the plans being presented to satisfy itself that the management development process within the department is being well managed and is in good hands.

We asked HR executives to tell us whether managers and executives whose performance or behavior is highly supportive of the management development policy were recognized and rewarded in their organizations. Disappointingly, only 46 percent of the respondents whose firms have a management development system said yes. If senior management fails to recognize good performance during the management development review, it is missing a real opportunity to motivate and encourage line management to take ownership and to further the process of management development.

FUNCTIONAL REVIEWS

At ARCO, we have movement between the HR functions at various operating companies, and some movement between HR and other functions. We believe that talent to run businesses comes from everywhere within the company—and management has a right to expect us to grow some of that talent in HR. We have an obligation to make a contribution—and we want the opportunity to do so.

James P. Brady, manager, HR Personnel Development, ARCO[8]

A question that frequently arises in management development discussions is "What are we developing this person for?" Is it so that the person can become a corporate general manager, general counsel, top HR executive, or corporate controller? The answer for each individual is based on background, qualifications, and desires. But clearly in the corporation there will be need for high-level functional management as well as for general management. The management development system should address both needs.

Where functional managers and non–operations professionals are on the payrolls of operating departments and subsidiaries, a functional review process may be implemented by the top corporate functional manager. (If these people are already on a headquarters functional payroll, then the functional review and department review, for that function, are one and the same.)

At times, the functional review process may seem to conflict with or be duplicative of the corporate line review process. However, the functional review gives professionals assurance that their particular expertise is not lost in the jungle of line operations and that they are in competition with like professionals. Several functions come to mind for which this may be true: information systems; financial; HR; law; medical; environmental; and public affairs.

Figure 7-2 illustrates the overlap between an HR functional review and an operating department review. There are usually HR people at the de-

FIGURE 7-2
Overlapping Functional Review and Operational Review Model

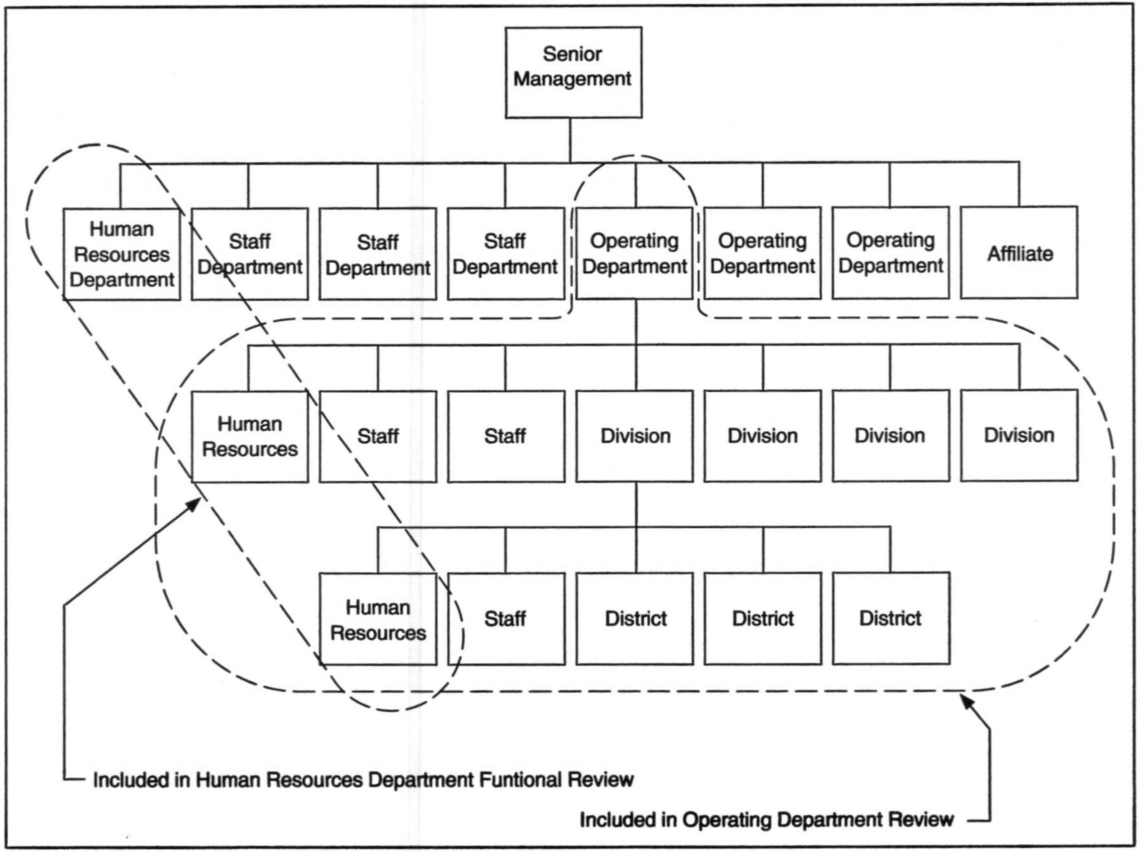

partment or division staff levels. A department manager would include the HR manager job on the department replacement tables and would talk about candidates for that job. Also, the department manager regards some HR personnel as having potential for line management and would discuss them in that light. Still, unless they are included in the functional HR review, HR people are not matched with future HR needs and opportunities outside the operating department.

For the functional review, the corporate HR manager establishes a review process, not unlike that established for the corporation by the CEO. The corporate HR manager will use his or her functional authority (dotted line) to have lower-level HR managers develop lists of high-potential candidates and their developmental plans. Then he or she will hold a review, probably with all of the next level of HR managers, to develop succession plans for HR jobs and agreement on high-potential candidates and their developmental plans.

In part, the functional review may be a defensive measure. The functional manager will want to defend his or her people and be sure that they are not overlooked in an operations-oriented competition. But for the review to be truly meaningful, there must be prior dialogue between the corporate HR manager and each of the line managers. The functional review helps ensure that individual employees will not be overlooked, that plans will be established for developing the expertise necessary for future management of the function, and that qualified functional candidates also can compete for line opportunities.

When the HR manager has the review with the senior management, he or she will discuss employees in the function as well as HR employees in operations and other units. He or she will probably include those field HR management jobs in the department's succession plans, although the responsibility for filling those jobs lies with line management. As we mentioned, there is redundancy. The same positions will be talked about in two different reviews.

PEOPLE, NOT POSITIONS

Management is tasks. Management is a discipline. But management is also people. Every achievement of management is the achievement of a manager. People manage rather than [do] "forces" or "facts."

Peter F. Drucker[9]

After years of experience with and as part of management development systems, it is crystal clear to us that the system should focus on individuals rather than on positions. Yet so much of what companies refer to as succession planning focuses on positions. Replacement charts show positions, and what is discussed is how to fill positions.

Of course, corporations must plan to fill positions. But we feel that succession plans will be improved if more energy is focused on individuals—knowing their strengths and weaknesses, knowing their desires, knowing their development needs. To some degree, succession plans evolve from individual development plans, but as a practical matter both plans are needed. This is why we encourage senior executives to structure management development reviews around discussions of people. Discussion of replacement tables should be secondary. Management can make final decision on replacements only when it fully understands the qualifications and readiness of the candidates. In the final analysis, judgments will be made about people, not positions.

We would like to believe that senior management sincerely wants everyone to succeed to his or her ultimate capabilities, to make the maximum contribution using both visible and untapped talents. By focusing on individuals in the management development reviews, senior management sets an example for managers at all levels. The key in management development is to have a system that forces the manager to make and take time to know employees and to give thought to the kinds of development that will be effective.

The focus on individuals starts with the senior-level review. Senior management can ask thoughtful questions about people:

- What do you think John expects in his next assignment?
- How do the people who work for Mary respond to her leadership?
- Why do you feel that Bob is not qualified to be the next district manager?
- What would it take to make Harry ready for your job?
- How will the advanced degree that Sue is working on help her in her career?

The department manager should have good answers for these questions. But in any event, he or she will go back and have more dialogue with subordinate managers and perhaps with the individuals discussed in the review. If the senior manager did not feel that the department manager had good answers, you can be sure the homework will be done the next time around.

PROCESS AT LOWER LEVELS

As we have shown, reviews can be held at different levels—corporate, operating company, department, and plant or division. Since the purpose of lower-level reviews is to develop information for the next level of review, the agendas are quite similar. To take one example, assume a production department consisting of a department manager, four staff managers, including HR, and five divisions.

The department manager has wide latitude to choose the format of the review. Possibly, he or she chooses an off-site, two-day meeting including the four staff managers and the division managers. Division managers will discuss their people, based on prior meetings with district managers, and identify those with high potential. There will be much discussion, during which views on potential will be challenged and defended. The managers will know most of the people being discussed and will have tried to get to know those who have been identified with high potential in the past. One goal will be to formulate a list of about 25 candidates considered to have potential to achieve senior-level management. A second list will also be developed mostly of younger employees who appear to have potential to go to the department manager level. Both lists will be ranked by potential (who would be most likely to achieve, next most likely, etc.).

Actual rankings are not as important as the thoughtful discussion that the exercise will produce. Following the meeting, the department manager will use the information gathered to develop replacement tables for the department and development plans for the highest potential employees. This work will involve heavy input from the department HR manager and discussion with other department managers on interfunctional moves.

The involvement of lower-level line managers in the management development process is fundamental to long-term success. In education, the value of a first-grade teacher is sometimes compared to the value of a high school math or science teacher. If salary is the measure of value, the high school teacher likely will win. But it is the first grade teacher who sets the foundation for the student's lifetime education. If the student starts out with a poor foundation, the high school teacher may not have much to work with.

So it is with younger employees. Their career foundations depend on knowledge imparted and developed by lower-level line managers. The opportunity for learning, growth, and development should not be wasted. A review system that forces line managers to participate in the early development of employees' careers will go a long way toward producing high-quality senior managers for the future. The major benefits of lower-level managers' involvement are:

1. Top-level succession and developmental plans will be built on a solid foundation.
2. Careers can be optimized for development by planning for them early.
3. A better, healthier dialogue between managers and subordinates improves employee retention.
4. The commitment of senior managers to management development will be much greater if they have had lengthy experience working with the company's system.

DOCUMENTATION AND FORMS

Documentation is kept to the minimum and we try to keep it very, very focused.

Walter R. Trosin, VP, Human Resources Merck[10]

The rule of thumb on documentation should be, "Less is more." Use no more than is absolutely necessary, and keep it as simple as possible. We offer the following cautions.

First, don't let the tail wag the dog! Documentation should serve the management development system, not the other way around. The scenario below may be all too typical of what happens.

Senior management decides it wants to get into succession planning and asks HR to design a program. Where does HR go for help? Perhaps it calls in several of the suppliers of succession planning software who will demonstrate programs that can document, update, perform searches, and incorporate "whistles and bells" at the wish of the HR manager. Before long HR has selected and purchased software and then starts to design the management development system around the software. By starting with the purchase of software, the project likely will not leave the ground!

Or possibly the company has an HR Information System (HRIS) in which it has invested heavily. Management and HR may feel obligated to go to HRIS for the design of a documentation system. Without having first determined what the goals of the management development system are to be, it will be difficult to design the computer information system to document it.

This is not to suggest that software should never be purchased or that HRIS should never be involved. But the basic planning for the management development system, including the review process, should be completed before the information system is designed.

Selecting software to meet a specific organizational need can be difficult at best. In May and June of 1989, *The HR Planning Newsletter*, published by Wargo & Co., provided a very useful comparison of six of the major software vendors in an article entitled "Succession Planning Software Shootout II." In view of the rapidly changing technology, a "Shootout III" would be timely and, we suspect, of great help to prospective users.

Second, documenting judgments can be tricky business, and too much documentation may be worse than too little. Poor quality or inaccuracy must be avoided, and training or orientation of managers in making judgments and filling out forms may be required.

Third, filling out forms is time-consuming and can be perceived by line management as a waste of time. The introduction of a new form—or even a new line on an existing form—should be made with great care and based on the value it adds to the program.

Fourth, basic employee information should be downloaded from HRIS into the management development system, not the other way around. Employee background, education, job history, and performance ratings are data that are useful for management development and should already exist in most HRIS data banks. Once it has been downloaded into a management development information system, it can be run separately on PCs. It is not desirable to load management development information into HRIS because it could give unintentional access to judgments and plans.

Documentation for the Senior-Level Review

Two key forms are required for the review itself: one for the succession plans (listing positions), and one for the developmental plans for high-potential individuals (listing people). These forms can be used at all levels so that the information is consistent and well understood. A third form, which details individual development plans for each high potential candidate, can be used as backup.

The key information that should be compiled on the succession planning form includes:

- Title of position
- Name of incumbent
- Names of replacements
- Ready now
- Ready in 2 years
- Ready in 3 or more years
- Five-year plan showing proposed changes

Eight to ten positions can be listed on one page, and comments should be limited to those having to do with the replacement plans and why one candidate is more likely to get the job than another. For incumbents and replacements some data on experience, potential, time in position, and so on, can be included, although this data should also be available from personal histories.

The information that should be compiled on the development planning form includes:

- Name
- Position
- Time in present assignment
- Proposed next position and date
- Proposed second position and date
- Ultimate potential — position

As many as 10 to 15 individuals can be shown on one sheet with the individual data and next two assignments all on one line. The next two assignments should cover at least five years and present a comparable time period to that given for the succession plans.

Information shown on the development planning form should be compatible with that on the succession planning form. For example, a "next assignment" on the developmental form should conform with a listing as a replacement on the succession planning form.

These two basic forms can be used to cover as many positions and people as is required for the review. In addition the same forms can be used for reviews at all levels.

Anyone who has worked with the forward plans (next two assignments) for high-potential candidates and then tried to harmonize those plans with the succession plans knows how difficult a three-dimensional project can sometimes be. The uncertainties of timing and other variables make the plans, particularly for the second assignment, tentative at best. However, it is our experience that such a planning exercise will result in better ultimate decisions and that the development plans will be more realistic.

Personal history information should be made available to the people sitting in on a review. As mentioned, individual personal history data sheets for each person mentioned in either plan can be included in the review book or package.

Most companies will use a separate form for each high-potential individual, giving comments and development plans. A typical form will include narratives on performance, potential, strengths and weaknesses, training needs, proposed assignments, and so forth and could be several pages long. These forms can serve as backup for the presenter at the review and are not distributed to the review committee members.

The narratives can cause problems. First, filling out forms can become a chore that encourages use of boilerplate language, which is not particularly useful. Another problem is lack of consistency. For example, a manager decides to give a negative comment on each individual to lend credibility and objectivity to his or her remarks. Unless all managers follow the same pattern, the individuals with negative comments could be perceived as having some real problems, or the negatives could be seen as having weight far beyond their true significance.

Since the people who will be discussed in a high-level review will be good, high performers, adjectives describing what a good, high performer should be are quite unnecessary. The documentation of strengths, weaknesses, and true problem areas or anomalies should address career impact and developmental needs rather than just general characteristics.

FEEDING BACK DOWN THE LINE

Whether minutes are prepared for the senior-level review will depend on the procedures being followed by the senior management. Minutes can be used to formalize specific decisions, including the acceptance of the succession and development plans. However, the plans themselves become the real documentation that can be referred to throughout the year.

Most of what is said behind the closed doors of the review session is for the information of the meeting participants only and need not be otherwise recorded. A department manager, upon returning from a senior-level review, may discuss the meeting with key staff and division managers who had participated in putting the plans together. No other feedback should be necessary. Still, many organizations do document specifics to reflect commitments made, actions agreed upon and the parties responsible, and to provide a paper trail for later evaluation.

If books were prepared for the senior-level review, then these can become the feedback as well as the working record of the succession and development plans. These "management development books" will be pulled out of the desks of the department and senior managers many times during the year.

Overall, management's deliberations at the senior-level review should be treated as highly confidential and not specifically referred to other than in discussion with the actual participants themselves. Of course, changes in plans and constructive suggestions for training and development should be passed down to managers directly responsible for taking developmental actions.

The question is often asked, "What should the employees named in the documentation be told after a formal review?" We posed this question to Steve McMahon, and these were his thoughts:

> You take your cues from the organization itself. The process ought to reflect the values of the organization. If it's an "open culture" then your succession planning process can be a little more open. If instead, it's a highly "closed culture," the process is going to be conducted on a more confidential basis, and there's probably not going to be a lot of feedback. If it's an open culture then I think you can give [an individual named in the plans] the feedback. My bias is, if you can't give feedback to individuals, what's the point. They don't know they're on the succession plan . . . and they may feel that they're being ignored or overlooked.[11]

We agree that it is important that a good employee know that he or she has not been ignored or overlooked. However, we would caution that we are talking about plans, not certainties, and that employees may not always understand the difference. It is a tough question, and we will offer some additional thoughts on feedback to employees in chapter 9.

CHAPTER CHECK LIST

The review process is not an end unto itself. It is a means to achieving a viable management development system. It is the core of such a system. Specifically the review process will:

1. Ensure that the management development process is functioning at all levels in the organization
2. Encourage a continuing management attention to the development of people
3. Encourage thoughtful, participatory judgments on the identification of potential and the planning for individual development
4. Communicate senior-level commitment down through the line organization
5. Provide input for staffing decisions consistent with the development of managers and the long-term needs of the corporation

The review process should be simple, relaxed, and nonbureaucratic. It should be basically the same at lower levels, and forms should be consistent. Some documentation is essential but should be kept to the necessary minimum.

Chapter Eight

ADDRESSING DIVERSITY

Managing diversity is an idea whose time has come. More and more, corporations and organizations of all kinds are awakening to the fact that a diverse work force is not a burden, but their greatest potential strength—when managed properly.

James E. Preston, CEO of Avon Products, Inc.[1]

WHO ARE WE TO SAY?

A chapter about diversity in the workplace that narrows in on the scarcity of women and minorities in the executive ranks is not likely to be well received by all readers. Women may feel that we, as males, cannot possibly understand the problems of subtle harassment and outright prejudice being faced by women who strive to advance in their organizations. Mothers could feel that we do not understand the problems of child care and home-making. Blacks may feel that we, as whites, do not understand that bigotry still exists in the workplace. Hispanics and Asians may believe that we do not appreciate the discrimination they face. White executives could feel that we do not fully understand the pressures of regulation and harassment by the government, the media, and special interest groups. And many white males may feel that we do not understand that they also are being discriminated against.

This is all correct to some degree. It is impossible for any one individual to fully understand the many complexities of this subject, and it is particularly impossible to empathize with people from so many different backgrounds and in so many different situations. But even without that full understanding, it seems clear that there is a need to achieve diversity in the executive ranks, whether it is in response to government pressure, corporate desire, or corporate need.

Our recommendations in this chapter will be based on five assumptions:

1. Age, gender, racial, and ethnic diversity in the executive ranks is a corporate strength, not a burden.
2. Many corporate managements truly want to achieve full diversity at all levels including executive.
3. The rate of progress to date has been too slow.
4. Prejudice still exists and makes the job of achieving diversity more difficult.
5. There are no inherent qualities of race or gender that affect the ability to lead or manage.

We will limit our comments to diversity as it applies to women and minorities in executive positions, although age, sexual preference, disability, geographical heritage, or even physical appearance also contribute to diversity.

A BIT OF HISTORY

Before deciding what can and should be done today to bring about diversity in the executive ranks, one must understand the history of antidiscrimination efforts. The concept of managing diversity is the culmination of a process that essentially began with Title VII of the Civil Rights Acts of 1964. Title VII established the Equal Employment Opportunity Commission to enforce prohibitions against discriminatory activity. At the time, civil rights was popularly associated with discrimination against blacks, but the Civil Rights Act has expanded to cover many kinds of discrimination—race, age, national origin, religion, sex, and physical disability.

Federal government involvement did not stop with the Civil Rights Act, however. Executive Order 11246 gave the government punitive power to cancel government contracts when vendors, suppliers, and contractors were found guilty of discrimination against protected classes. This was a big stick held over the vast number of corporations that depended on government contracts for some portion of their revenue. Revised Order No. 4 added the requirement that affirmative action be taken where the government determined that imbalances of race or gender existed.

Add to these regulations the Age Discrimination Act, the Equal Pay Act of 1963 (addressing gender-based salary inequities), and the Rehabilitation Act of 1973 (addressing discrimination against the handicapped). The whole process of recruitment, hiring, promotion, demotion, and termination is now subject to numerous federal government requirements. Government regulation has created a new field of specialized knowledge and expertise for both the public and private sectors.

Corporate Response

Prior to the 1970s, discrimination was blatant, and many corporate executives had difficulty in accepting that discrimination was wrong. Racial prejudice existed in the executive offices as well as on the assembly line. Women were not considered as candidates for managerial and many professional jobs. Although many executives began to examine corporate personnel practices from a moral or ethical point of view, most did little until they were threatened with legal sanctions. It was easy to rationalize that the absence of minorities and women in professional and management jobs was the fault of something other than corporate prejudice.

Efforts to reduce discrimination against blacks was the first corporate response in the mid-1960s. The inferior and segregated educational system to which blacks were consigned did not equip them for business and industry. Yet responsible corporations, to comply with hiring quotas that were being suggested by the federal government, turned to recruiting at the predominantly black colleges. Even when quotas were met, the new black employees had two strikes against them. First was the prejudice of fellow employees; second, and more important, was the difficulty of competing armed with what, for most, was an inferior education.

Another obstacle to integrating blacks in corporations was the corporate *perception* of public opinion. The suggestion that customers might not buy from a black sales representative virtually excluded blacks from opportunities in marketing. It took courage to test those waters, and fortunately many black employees—and corporations as well—had that courage. There are, no doubt, many examples similar to that of the black sales representative assigned in the late 1960s to a rural Louisiana territory by a major oil company. Important customers threatened to boycott the company. The company stood firm, as did the sales representative, who must have felt enormous personal pressure.

The federal government broadened its civil rights enforcement to include Hispanics, Native Americans, and Asians. Putting all minorities under the same umbrella may have been unfortunate, since the nature of discrimination against each minority group is quite different and the problems vary greatly by geography.

Discrimination against women was an accepted practice by most corporations prior to civil rights legislation. Women were welcome in the workplace—as secretaries, receptionists, clerks, and nonskilled production line employees. However, in spite of the progress made in hiring women into professional positions, prejudice still exists against women in executive roles. With opportunities now more available, many women are taking the necessary steps to become qualified for technical and business careers, a drastic change from a few decades ago. (To note the improvement, women made up 31 percent of the entering class in 1991 for the College of Engineering at Cornell University!)[2]

Still, male chauvinists continue to maintain that women should not be executives. "They are not assertive enough. They are not sufficiently committed. They are too emotional." Of course, the relatively few women who have become senior executives—many by heading up their own businesses—seriously challenge these arguments.

The phrase "the glass ceiling" has been coined to describe the invisible barrier to the advancement of women (and minorities) above a certain level in the organization. Does such a barrier actually exist? Is the glass ceiling created by prejudice rather than the result of the lack of qualified candidates? We believe that a barrier does exist and that prejudice is still a problem. There are fewer qualified candidates in general but it results, in part, from the failure of business to provide developmental opportunities and experiences that feed the management pipeline, thus implicating prejudice as the primary culprit.

Our view is supported by a U.S. Department of Labor study, released in August 1991, on promotional practices at nine large corporations. The study found that women and minorities were not given crucial early training and that they were frequently passed over for the high-visibility special projects that could let them make their mark.[3]

In June 1991, *Business Week* and Louis Harris & Associates surveyed 404 senior executives concerning corporate progress on equal opportunity measures.[4] Business leaders gave themselves pretty good marks, and the majority expressed the view that government pressure was not needed. However, 53 percent felt that companies needed to do a better job of hiring, training, and promoting minorities, and 44 percent felt the need to do a better job in the hiring, training, and promoting of women. A significant but not surprising result was the low mark given to corporate efforts to promote women and minorities into top management.

We consider the response to this survey to be encouraging. As we said in chapter 5, the commitment and involvement of senior management is necessary before a process of management development will really work. However, commitment must be turned into action if corporate America is to diversify its executive ranks.

Lesson from History

1. Civil rights legislation and government enforcement have brought about, to a great degree, a diversified workforce in many corporations. This is a very positive change. It may have occurred over time with evolving corporate morality, but clearly government has influenced the rate of progress.
2. Elevating workforce diversity to executive levels is the challenge of the 1990s. It will take continued action by CEOs to propel organizations forward.
3. The progress that has taken place over the past 20 years is only the beginning of what is needed to fully overcome prejudice and to bring about full diversity in the executive ranks.

DIVERSITY IS A BUSINESS NEED

Affirmative action is not just the right thing to do. It's a business necessity.

                              Robert E. Allen, Chairman, AT&T[5]

We would like to believe that today, executives accept and evaluate each employee as an individual, without regard to race or gender. Yet that is not always the case. It is clear, however, that increased workforce diversity will be achieved at all levels when corporate managements see this as a means of achieving long-term business objectives rather than as a response to government inspection.

The Demographic Reality

According to a recent survey of Fortune 1000 companies released by the Labor Department,[6] only 6.6 percent of executive positions are filled by women and 2.6 percent by minorities. (Because of the fuzziness over the definition of "executive," the actual percentages of women and minorities in true executive positions is probably much lower.) The call to accelerate the upward flow of women and minorities is a matter of supply and demand. Government interest in and enforcement of equal employment opportunity (EEO) will not go away, but the compelling need is to assure long-range business success, not produce numbers for the government inspector nor to counter an EEO charge or suit.

Based on demographics, it seems clear that over the next two or three decades, the pool that will supply the executive ranks will consist of an increasing percentage of women and minorities.[7] The upward flow of women and minorities must accelerate to assure that a diverse workforce is equipped to compete for management and executive positions.

Don't Forget the Customers

Customers for most products and services are as diverse as the population. Companies operating on a global basis will serve customers of even greater cultural diversity. For example, a glance at other drivers on the freeway in rush-hour traffic would reveal that car drivers (and buyers) are not limited to one gender, race, or age. The car-buying public is truly diverse!

There are two implications for customer diversity as it relates to diversity in the executive ranks. First, there will be a higher level of understanding of the customer where the same diversity exists among executive decision-makers. With better understanding, management will do a better job in meeting the customer needs. Second, customers who are angry about or disappointed in the lack of diversity in the executive ranks of suppliers will direct their buying power accordingly.

RECRUITMENT AND SELECTION

The first step in the process of executive development is recruitment. Based on current population demographics, corporations are already recruiting from a more diversified population, and this will intensify. Yet although the percentage of minorities is increasing, the minorities considered qualified (for professional entry-level jobs) remain in short supply. On the other hand, the supply of qualified women in most professional areas is good, and the business challenge is to assure that the same selection criteria are being applied for both men and women. More simply stated, any vestige of prejudice should be eliminated in recruiting.

The education system is not doing the job for minorities. Unless education trends improve and the problems of poverty in the inner cities are resolved, minorities will remain underrepresented in all levels of the corporate ranks. The Los Angeles riots in the spring of 1992 would indicate that these problems are far from resolved. Assuming the general validity of the SAT for the moment, SAT scores released by the College Board in 1991 do not bode well for the future. The average total score has fallen in each of the last four years.[8] In particular, the math mean scores show a dismal picture of black students' educational preparation.[9]

Black	385
Puerto Rican	406
Mexican American	427
Other Hispanic	431
White	489
Asian	530

These data would support the general belief that many blacks and Hispanics remain educationally disadvantaged, while Asians are taking full advantage of educational opportunity. Asians did not do as well as whites on the verbal test, possibly reflecting language difficulties, but they did considerably better than each of the three Hispanic groups and blacks.

The debate over the role of the historically black colleges and universities continues, and corporations must decide on the level of recruiting efforts at those schools. *Time* magazine featured an article entitled "Are Black Colleges Worth Saving?" in which it was pointed out that the problems faced by black public colleges were created, and in the past supported, under the doctrine of separate but equal.[10] Business must concern itself with the problems being faced by minorities who depend on public education and must play a greater role in the improvement of that educational system.

Suggestions for Recruiting Minorities

Invest in the education system for the disadvantaged. The highest priority for developing blacks to become executives must be in the recruitment and selection of truly qualified candidates who will be able to compete on their own merits. Corporate America must continue affirmative action efforts to bring more blacks into an educational system that will qualify them to compete in industry. Corporate investment of money and talent in the precollege education system will detract minimally from short-term profits, and it will have a leveraged, positive impact on corporate America in the next 10 to 20 years. It is a hard investment to make, but one that is strongly needed. The job is not being done by the public sector.

Use role models to demonstrate opportunity. Industry needs to demonstrate that opportunity *does* exist for blacks in the management and executive ranks. Professional sports has developed role models and demonstrated that there are opportunities for black athletes. Industry, on the other hand, has relatively few black executive role models, but it should aggressively use those few individuals to show that opportunity exists for all races and genders.

Xerox Corporation proves that the use of black role models does work. Nine percent of its top 196 managers are black versus a national average of about .5 percent of top managers. At Xerox, a black caucus referred to as "the Black Network" has existed, with corporate encouragement, for many years. It supplies a combination of support, counsel, self-help, and encouragement to black employees.[11]

Set high standards for academic performance. Business should take advantage of the selection process that already occurs at the college level. If a university has an affirmative action program designed to bring academically qualified minorities to its institution, then the odds of recruiting qualified employees will be much higher than at an institution that places little emphasis on quality. Emphasis on high academic standards can have a positive ripple effect on the entire educational system.

Avoid "tokenism." Candidates should know that they are being selected based on their qualifications, not race. Although showcasing and tokenism may be things of the past, candidates will be most sensitive to any suggestion that they are not being considered based on their individual talents and abilities. Unfortunately there are still many recruiters and managers whose careless or insensitive remarks can cause the corporation to lose the consideration of a highly qualified individual.

SOME SPECIAL CHALLENGES FOR GENDER DIVERSITY

The career models for many college-trained professional women are mothers who were happy as homemakers. It is not totally unexpected, then, that some percentage of working professional women ultimately will follow the career paths of their mothers and drop out of the workforce before moving up in the managerial ranks. But the professional woman today has corporate opportunities that were not available to her mother. Challenge, prestige, and money will compete with the desire to spend time with her children and care for her family. Many women will compromise. They will continue their careers, but raise their children by relying on the additional services that are available. However, as many employed mothers have found, it is anything but easy.

What Can Corporations Do?

Corporations must first recognize that the stereotypical career development process may present many obstacles to women who want also to fulfill the role of mother and homemaker. In the past, corporations have tended to write off such a candidate, perceiving that she had chosen her family over her career. Corporations must seek out creative and innovative ways to make the two careers compatible, or a vast reservoir of executive talent will go untapped.

Corporations must also diligently and continually communicate a strong position against gender bias. This includes *actions* by senior executives as well as policies declaring the corporation's intention to advance women to the executive level. Strategies for accomplishing the advancement of women should be communicated throughout the company. Further, corporations must make exceptional efforts to move women into line management positions and not allow them to just drift into public affairs, HR, and other staff roles because it is easier and women might be more readily accepted. Denying women line management experience puts them at an almost insurmountable disadvantage in the competition for senior executive positions.

Corporations should listen to what women themselves have to say through focus groups, task forces, and other forums for communication. Finally, they must explore ways to make the corporation more "family friendly."

Felice Schwartz, the founder and president of CATALYST, a not-for-profit organization that works with corporations to foster the career growth of women, offers more specific advice to CEOs in the *Harvard Business Review*. She names four strategies for clearing the path to the top for "career primary" women:

1. Identify them early.
2. Give women the same opportunity you give to talented men to grow and develop and contribute to company profitability. Give them client and customer responsibility. Expect women to travel, relocate and make the same commitment to the company as men in aspiring leadership positions.
3. Accept women as valued members of your management team. Include them in every kind of communication. Listen to them.
4. Recognize that the business environment is more difficult and stressful for them than for their male peers.[12]

The Unique Problems of Dual-Career Families

A societal change of great impact on succession planning and management development is the increase in the number of dual-income families. The historical model for executive development was a male breadwinner whose wife and children were free to follow the employee to a new assignment.

The dual-career family upsets that model as well as the corporation's ability to relocate employees for advancement and development. In more and more families, women are as likely as their husbands to have the dominant career. We offer the following guidelines that can be applied in the design of succession planning and career development systems:

1. A spouse's career must be considered as an important variable, but one that is to be managed by the employee, not the organization.
2. Corporations should try to assist spouses in obtaining a new position. Obviously, each situation is different and the corporate resources are

limited. However, the intent may be fulfilled even by timing the job change in consideration of the spouse's needs. Stated another way, the corporation should recognize, not run away from, the problem.

3. The same assistance to spouses should be considered equally for male and female employees.

4. Hiring a spousal "team" may compound executive development decisions. When relocating an employee, the corporation has responsibility to both spouses, and this may complicate the selection of the best developmental assignments. Further, it is unlikely that each spouse's career will move at the same pace, and the corporation—not the employees—will be making the decision on which is the dominant provider. Hiring spouses can work well, but it is important that both employees understand there may be trade-offs.

5. In view of the greater total income, a dual-income employee may perceive that he or she has more options and be less willing to relocate or even accept a particular assignment. This places a greater burden on the organization to choose meaningful and challenging assignments that will further the employee's career, while accomplishing the business objectives of the organization.

The Challenge of Child Care

For a working parent, the need for child care is a major concern at all job levels. The likelihood that an executive will be subjected to less regular working hours and more business travel than many professional employees just makes the problem more difficult. In fairness, however, the employer can be expected to do no more for the executive than for a clerical employee. So child care must be addressed for the total workforce.

A caring organization readily understands that children are a top priority of its employees (male or female). The organization should be flexible in allowing employees to tend to family emergencies (including aging parents as well as children).

Child care that is convenient to the workplace allows parents to quickly visit children in emergencies or even at lunch time. DuPont is one of the leaders in addressing this very important need of working parents. DuPont has paid out $1.5 million over three years to build and renovate child care centers near its major work sites around the country.[13]

Johnson & Johnson is another "family friendly" corporation that has child care programs among other family-sensitive initiatives.[14] According to

Management Review, at Johnson & Johnson the work and family commitment is so strong that the company has changed its official corporate credo to include the statement "We must be mindful of ways to help employees fulfill their family responsibilities."[15]

Moreover, providing child care, along with elder care, is being recognized by informed, progressive organizations as a competitive advantage in the 1990s. Hugh McColl, CEO of NationsBank, Charlotte, North Carolina, expressed his views this way: "Anyone who ignores the challenges and conflicts inherent in the current work-family issues will ultimately pay a huge price in turnover, lost time, and general disenchantment with the company. We don't plan to let that happen to us."[16]

Job Sharing

Organizations must continue to search for creative ways to utilize professional women's talents and to help them prepare for later careers, even during the years when they may opt to stay at home with the children. We do not suggest that a woman working part time will remain fully competitive with an employee devoting all of his or her time to the job. But we do believe that corporations should seek ways to utilize and nurture employees' talents rather than to abandon them.

Job sharing is one alternative. Alan Deutschman describes a typical arrangement:

> Often both sharers work three days every week creating an overlap day for extended face-to-face conferencing. Companies typically pay the two a total of 120% of what one person would make in the job and in response the duo may take on some responsibilities beyond the original job description.[17]

This is not a radical departure from staffing with only full-time positions when considering that with traditional staffing, many responsibilities are shared anyway to keep the business running, and usually there is more than one individual qualified to handle a problem or make a decision. Few executives remain behind their desks every day of the week!

Felice N. Schwartz has concluded: "I believe ... that shared employment is the most promising and will be the most widespread form of flexible scheduling in the future."[18]

Work at Home

With the advent of the personal computer and modem, responsible work can be fully completed at home. Except for the traditional view that employees should be at their desks, many professional employees could perform their responsibilities with a telephone and computer tied into the corporate network.

Kay is an example of how an employee can function productively without going to the office. She is a sales manager for a medical services company with a territory covering several midwestern states, and she operates from her home, some 250 miles from the corporate office. When she travels in her territory, her office goes with her. She plugs the hotel room telephone line into her portable computer and is in immediate communication with the entire corporate network, just as she is when at home. Kay's schedule and hours vary greatly, but she is valued not by the hours she works but by the results she produces. She is part of a dual-career family, and her talent would be lost if her employer required her to relocate and work from the headquarters office.

Marilyn resigned from her corporate position in HR when she decided that caring for her baby was her top priority. It was a loss to the corporation because of Marilyn's specialized knowledge and experience. Finally an arrangement was worked out where Marilyn could work from her home, using a computer tied into the office, on her own part-time schedule. Not only was this a mutually beneficial short-term arrangement, but the day may come when Marilyn's children are older and she is anxious to resume her career full-time. If the corporation can maintain this part-time relationship over the years, Marilyn may again return to fulfill a greater corporate need.

According to Felice Schwartz, "Part-time employment is the single greatest inducement to getting women back on the job expeditiously, and the provision women themselves most desire."[19]

Progressive employers, today, are providing such arrangements for employees who are extremely valuable but may be confined to home for child care or even personal illness. It is done out of business necessity. What we are suggesting is that such arrangements be considered on a proactive basis for parents who would be willing to continue to work part-time, but who would resign or go on leave rather than come to the office daily.

Flex Time

Flex time can be useful in enabling parents of young children to contribute and to be developed for executive roles. Unfortunately, for most managerial and executive positions, the hours of expected availability may discourage the following of fixed schedules. In terms of pure job requirements, however, the more senior the position, the more control the incumbent has over his or her work schedule. Again, we suggest that flex time be considered on a proactive basis, recognizing the needs of the specific job, to assist young mothers and fathers in handling child care.

Personal Leave

It has been well demonstrated that women can take time off to have children and return, fully productive, to the job. Likewise, men have remained productive after serious illness or assignments on special projects. As the length of the leave increases, however, it becomes more difficult to say that the career is not being adversely impacted. A prolonged absence from the job certainly affects one's ability to compete. However, although a career may be slowed down, it need not be abandoned altogether.

We think that the corporation should provide reasonable career protection for women on maternity leave. In fact, it must, if it intends to have gender diversity among its executives. Further, we suggest that corporations consider women who are on indefinite leaves (maybe as long as several years) as resources not to be abandoned. It means remaining in touch and continuing to pursue avenues of part-time work as was done in the Marilyn example mentioned above.

WHEN AFFIRMATIVE ACTION BECOMES NEGATIVE ACTION

I am proposing that managing diversity be used along with affirmative action in the short run. In the long run, effective implementation of managing diversity will make affirmative action unnecessary. Unfortunately, at our present pace, the long run may be 20 to 25 years.

R. Roosevelt Thomas, Executive Director,
The American Institute for Managing Diversity.[20]

Roosevelt Thomas is right. Affirmative action is needed to make up for lost time, but the ultimate goal is to achieve executive diversity through normal developmental processes. And as Thomas ably points out, it will take years to reach that goal.

Unfortunately, for some HR practitioners, affirmative action is reduced entirely to quantitative terms to be plugged into the goals and timetables scrutinized by EEO inspectors. This, of course, creates a perception of special treatment and reverse discrimination, which is unfortunate for both the minority and majority employee.

> **When quotas and preferential treatment are the thrust of affirmative action, it is no longer affirmative, but instead becomes negative.**

In managerial development and promotion, affirmative action should not result in preferential treatment. Rather it is a threefold commitment to:

1. Help people who have been disadvantaged to gain the skills, knowledge, experience, and confidence to compete on an equal basis.
2. Prevent bias and discrimination by communicating the corporate commitment and providing training where necessary.
3. Establish an accountability process to assure that the developmental needs of minorities and women are being addressed by management throughout the organization.

Helping People to Become Qualified

Affirmative action is applied to identifying the needs of members of protected classes and helping them to better *qualify* themselves to compete on an equal basis with white males. Help to the disadvantaged is most beneficial when it is applied to early education, as already mentioned. However, there are things that can be done within the workforce. For example, job-related and interpersonal skills training should be made available to *all* employees. The affirmative action will be in assuring that minorities who need such training actually receive it. Mentoring, an informal process, should be made available to all professional employees, but particular attention should be given to how mentors can help women and minorities advance. The network of black managers and executives at Xerox

Corporation provides mentors for black employees.[21] The ideal mentor, generally, however, is the immediate or "one level up" supervisor. Assigning special projects that will give broader exposure to individuals and the opportunity to gain self-confidence is also helpful. This should be available to all employees. However, minority and female employees may have a greater need for this assistance.

Reducing Bias

There are four keys to reducing bias within the workforce.

1. Senior executives set an example.

While it is naive to think bias will ever be completely eliminated, the first step is for senior executives to demonstrate that they personally have full and equal respect for all human beings. Senior management must work hard to assure that there are no barriers, no glass ceilings. Care should be taken throughout the organization to assure that gender-based or racially based innuendos or slurs are not tolerated.

2. Communicate the corporate commitment.

The communication of corporate commitment may not eliminate prejudice, but it can help eliminate discrimination. Reuben Mark, chair of Colgate-Palmolive, says it well: "The pressure has to come from the top. The organization reacts to what management values, whether it is profits or strong cultural diversity."[22]

3. Discipline managers and employees who discriminate or reflect their personal prejudices.

It does no good for the CEO to state a corporation position on equality and then have managers and employees act contrary to that position by making racial or sexual slurs, inappropriate comments, or other actions reflecting bias. This is not to take away the right of individual belief, but it does take away the right to discriminate in the workplace when that act is contrary to the corporate commitment and that commitment is morally and legally justified.

4. Work to build understanding and harmony in the workforce.

Cross-cultural training has been effectively used by many corporations, and there is a variety of material, including videos, available for in-house training courses. Although much has been accomplished, the job is far from finished. Other good things are beginning to happen. The diversity that now exists (although not at executive levels) is providing an ongoing opportunity for employees from all groups to understand cultural differences. Biased attitudes are often learned unconsciously, and they can be unlearned. As we work day-to-day with people and get to know them as individuals, cultural biases begin to dissolve.

Although the problems of prejudice and bias have not been solved, they are being recognized and efforts are ongoing to solve them. *Workforce America! Managing Employee Diversity As a Vital Resource* by Marilyn Loden and Judy B. Rosener[23] is a good example of a useful resource for identifying problems and solutions. It, as well as many other timely books and articles, should be of help to those responsible for furthering the cross-cultural training efforts within corporations.

ESTABLISHING ACCOUNTABILITY

When senior management has clarified its position on the advancement of women and minorities into management positions, it must then take positive steps to identify and develop candidates who currently are at lower levels. There are two primary tools for doing this, the review process and documentation.

The Review Process

Include on the agenda of the annual succession planning and executive development review with each department the specific subject of the development of women and minorities. The important thing is to have the topic discussed by the reporting manager so that senior management can be assured that women and minorities in each organization are being identified and developed.

Knowing that you will be engaged in dialogue with senior management on the subject will do much to assure that you are prepared. The reporting manager will have done his or her homework. He or she will have discussed with subordinates, in great detail, the individual women and minorities in the organization. The reporting manager should, if possible, arrange to meet and know those persons indicated to have high potential. And he or she will discuss developmental needs and what is being or needs to be done about them.

The scheduled review with a department manager will generate detailed reviews at lower levels. Since the primary tool in executive development is the thoughtful judgment of managers, putting the development of women and minorities on the executive development review agenda will create a focus of thoughtful judgments on those individuals.

At the senior-level review of the department, the manager will talk from the forms. But probably more importantly, he or she will be questioned by senior management. Typical questions about women might be:

- Who are the three highest potential women (or black or Hispanic) employees? ... And then for each,
- What is her next planned assignment?
- What might limit her potential?
- What is being done to better prepare her for future assignments?
- What special projects can you use to give her more developmental experience and exposure to senior management?
- What are her career aspirations?
- Why are there so few high-potential women in your organization?
- Is the corporation recruiting the right individuals?
- What unique problems do women in your department face, and what is being done to address them?

The purpose of such questions is not so much to elicit specific information as it is to engage the manager in thoughtful dialogue and to demonstrate corporate commitment to the advancement of women and minorities throughout the organization.

As part of the review discussion, senior management may commend or criticize the actions being reported on. Either reaction will demonstrate that senior management is serious. For certain, the subject will gain more ongoing attention in the year to follow. It is recommended that the development of women and minorities be listed separately on the agenda and not be grouped together under the same heading for the discussion.

Documentation

We offer samples of two forms that can be used for documentation. One lists women (or minorities) with basic data and the next likely assignment with date. See Figure 8-1. The other is an individual developmental form similar to that used for all high-potential employees. See Figure 8-2.

FIGURE 8-1
High Potential List

Category: Women
Department: Manufacturing
Date: 2/2/92

Name (Date Hired)	Perf /Pot	Present Position (level)	Date	Estimated Next Position (level)	Est. Date	Estimated Highest Position (level)	Years to Achieve
Susan Randall (6/90)	B/24	Quality Assurance Specialist (16)	7/91	Supv.— Packaging (17)	2/93	Plant Manager (24)	18

FIGURE 8-2
Development Plan

NAME:	Susan Randall	Date Hired 6/90

DEPARTMENT: Manufacturing

EDUCATION: B Mech Engr   Purdue University   1990

Performance / Potential: B / 24

Present Position: Quality Assurance Specialist   Date: 7/91

Strengths for Achieving Potential:

　　—Has a clear bias for action.
　　—Possesses a good orientation to:
　　　　Continuous improvement
　　　　Quality Assurance
　　　　Customer service

Obstacles to Achieving Potential:

　　—Does not seem comfortable when senior management is around.
　　—Oral presentation skills.
　　—Interpersonal skills, particularly in managing conflict.

Recommended Actions:

　　—Attend "Conflict Resolution" program.
　　—Enroll in next course "Making Presentations"
　　—Invite her to participate in more management meetings involving quality
　　　　assurance and customer service.
　　—Promote to supervisor within a year but follow immediately with "New
　　　　Supervisors" training course.

PREPARED BY: Joe Henry   TITLE: Quality Supv   DATE: 1/25/92

Figure 8.1 can be used to list all professional/managerial women, or only a limited number can be listed (for example, the list could be of the 10 highest potential women, or those already at a certain level). The manager should be prepared to discuss each person listed. This kind of form can be restricted to one organization, but having several key items helps generate useful discussion. Most important are the entries for the next position and the estimated highest position along with the estimated dates for attaining. The manager will come to the review prepared to discuss potential plans and specific developmental needs, not generalities. The form is used to establish accountability as well as to provoke thoughtful judgments.

Figure 8.2 is one form that can be used to indicate an individual's strengths, weaknesses, and developmental plans. It is a working tool and backup to Figure 8.1. Its value comes not so much from the specific documentation, but from the thought processes that it requires. It is senior management's decision whether such a form should be presented and discussed on each individual. A similar form should be used for all high-potential employees.

This Is Not Reverse Discrimination

Having specific reviews of women and minorities does not discriminate against white males. In most cases today, the preponderance of the people listed and reviewed in the executive development process are still white males. Singling out women and minorities for special discussion should have two very positive effects, neither of which is adverse to the interest of white males:

1. The message will be communicated to lower-level managers that the corporation is truly committed to diversity.
2. There will be continuous efforts to better qualify women and minorities to compete.

DIVERSITY CHECK LIST

1. Has your firm kept up with historical progress?
   a. What percentage of recent college hires have been:

- Black?
- Hispanic?
- Asian?
- Women?

b. What percentage of executives in the top three corporate levels are:
- Black?
- Hispanic?
- Asian?
- Women?

c. How committed is senior management to achieving diversity in the executive ranks?
- Through example in discussion and interpersonal relationships?
- Through clear communication of the corporate commitment?

d. Does the workforce accept diversity?
- Are acts or accusations of prejudice or harassment immediately investigated and disciplined if substantiated?
- Are there any indications that minorities or women are uncomfortable in the workforce?

2. What cross-cultural training exists in your firm to better sensitize supervisors and employees to culture and gender differences?

3. What actions are being taken to improve the quality of college graduates, particularly minorities?
   a. Working with colleges and universities to help them attract better qualified candidates
   b. Working with inner-city schools to motivate students to aspire to a college education and professional employment
   c. Using minority role models to inspire youth

4. What actions are being taken to improve the recruitment of qualified minorities?
   a. Setting high standards for academic performance
   b. Using role models to demonstrate corporate opportunity
   c. Having all employees who will talk to recruits sensitive to the importance of considering the individual without regard to race or gender

5. Are supervisors and managers accountable for the development of women and minorities?
   a. Do managers review high-potential women and minorities with senior management on at least an annual basis?

   b. Are the development plans for these people documented?

6. Are actions by the organization directed toward qualifying women and minorities to compete for advancement rather than giving preferential treatment in promotions?

7. Are corporate policies and practices sensitive to the problems of child care, single parents, and dual-career families?

Chapter Nine

ASSESSING POTENTIAL

A ssessing potential is a subject that seems to generate great interest and attention in any discussion of succession planning and management development. It is a difficult subject to address because of the complexity of the issues it raises. For example:

- Is potential based on actual performance or on intrinsic characteristics?
- Is potential inherent, and to what extent can it be developed or changed?
- Is potential a function of behavior or of competencies?
- By what process should judgments be made?
- To what degree should scientific tools be used in assessment?

In this chapter we will talk about assessing employees' long-range potential rather than assessing potential for immediate promotion. The techniques may be the same, but the objectives are quite different. For purposes of management development, assessment means identifying candidates with the potential to advance several levels and doing it so that there is time to provide the experiences required to fulfill that highest potential in an orderly fashion. By contrast, assessments that have the objective of selecting candidates are usually short-term actions taken to meet immediate needs.

We will discuss two aspects of assessment. First, process—the mechanics and procedures for accomplishing assessments throughout the organization. Then we will discuss the techniques for making individual judgments.

THE ASSESSMENT PROCESS

We believe that the assessment process should:

- Establish uniform definitions of potential, either by job level or by specific position

- Train managers in the art of assessment to assure a uniform approach
- Force managers to know their employees and to assess their potential by understanding their work and talking with them
- Engage managers in a dialogue with their peers and supervisors in which they must defend decisions on potential
- Be repeated annually

A Zero-Base Process

Much of what we consider in assessing potential is inherent in the individual. It is likely that successful senior executives today received praise from their teachers. Their accomplishments in high school would likely have been noteworthy as would have been their accomplishments in college and perhaps the military. And their selection in the recruitment process would have revealed not only academic accomplishment, but some evidence of leadership.

Then why do we say that potential assessment should be zero-base (a new evaluation each year) when potential is inherent? Here are four reasons:

1. People change.

There are late bloomers and people who fail to live up to their potential as they take on more responsibility. Admittedly, there will be a continuing "halo" effect once someone has been accepted as having high potential, but the system should not encourage that automatic assessment.

2. Employees deserve more than one chance to demonstrate their potential.

It can be devastating to an employee to feel that the die has been cast and there is nothing further that can be done to earn consideration for promotion.

3. Some good people will be overlooked and lost.

Assessment in most companies is more art than science; individuals with exceptional potential will be easily recognized. But many others, who have the potential to fill needed roles in the organization, may be overlooked if assessment is just a one-time exercise.

4. Potential also reflects available opportunity.

Management needs are constantly changing as is the number of available candidates, all of which may redefine an individual's potential.

Admittedly, we are walking a fine line. On the one hand, we say that the people who have potential have had it from an early age and it is easy to recognize. On the other hand, we say that potential may be a latent quality or one that will be developed over time. We believe that both statements are true. The effort to make assessment a continuing process of reevaluation rather than a one-time effort is healthy for the organization and fair to the entire workforce.

Procedural Model

Figure 9-1 shows the engineering department in a hypothetical organization. We would suggest the following annual procedure for assessing the potential of the 40 engineers in the organization's four sections.

Step 1.   Each of four section supervisors assesses the potential of the 10 engineers and places them in rank order by potential. Four levels of potential are used: (1) above department manager; (2) department manager; (3) section supervisor; and (4) no further potential.

Step 2.   Section supervisors meet with department manager and staff manager, as an ad hoc committee, to develop a composite ranking for all 40 engineers. Developing this ranking involves discussion—challenging and defending—to bring out the best thinking of the supervisors. Supervisors, knowing that they will have to defend their decisions to peers as well as to the boss, will have given much thought to their decisions.

Step 3.   Department manager will discuss the top 10 candidates at the next level of review, along with comments on future assignments and developmental needs.

The next review level probably would consist of the other managers in the services group along with the senior vice president. In addition to discussing the highest potential engineers, the engineering manager would present an assessment of potential and ranking of his or her five direct

FIGURE 9-1
Procedural Model for Assessment

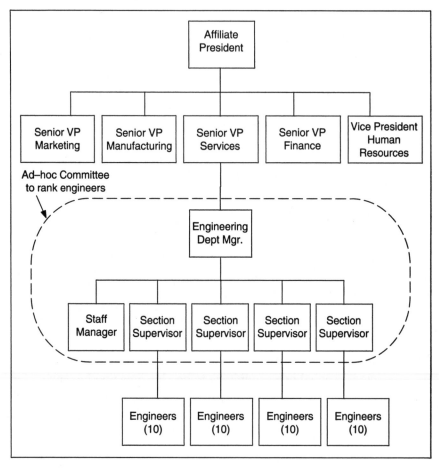

subordinates as well as the succession plans for those positions. As we mentioned in chapter 7, the review process would be essentially the same at this and the next higher level.

Benefits of Ranking

We believe that the ranking by potential encourages the manager doing the ranking to expend "thinking" energy. It takes better understanding to say that Employee X is more likely to reach department manager than

Employee Y than it does to say that X has potential to become department manager. Possibly the greatest benefit in ranking by a team or committee comes from the review and discussion of all employees, even those who do not make the high-potential list. It is a means of assuring that no one is being overlooked and provides checks and balances against biased or misinformed judgments.

Identifying the Very Highest Potential Candidates

No value is served by placing a very high potential rating on a candidate within the first few years of service. In our example, the engineers at the lowest level need to be assessed based on the potential to move no more than two or three levels. Candidates at the section supervisor level, who have had opportunity to demonstrate some management skills, could be assigned higher potentials.

The early identification of very high potential is of value only if and when a career must be altered to accommodate that faster track. However, in the early years, the emphasis will be on learning the grass-roots business, and the track would be substantially the same for all higher management candidates. In chapter 10 we will discuss a career-path model leading to CEO. In our model, the decision point for CEO versus lower management potential would not occur sooner than at least 10 to 12 years of service.

Forced Distribution

To some degree, the fact that there are few opportunities per candidate makes it practical to limit the number of employees identified as having very high potential. At some point, senior management will be grappling with the career plans and development of the high-potential candidates, and it serves the process better to keep the number of candidates manageable as well as realistic. However, with the benefit of an annual review cycle, the list can change slightly from year to year. An organization of tens of thousands of employees might have a list of only 20 to 25 people carrying the very highest corporate potential. In turn, each department may have 20 to 25 people listed as having department-head potential. Totaling the department head lists for the entire corporation would result in a next-cut list of a hundred or more candidates. As one moves further down the hierarchy of the organization, several hundred employees may be reviewed on high-potential lists.

Forms

Should "potential" forms be filled out by the manager on each individual? It may not be necessary if development needs and plans are documented as part of the appraisal package. If the appraisal form provides this documentation, filling out additional forms may be "make-work" for the manager unless it elicits a more thoughtful judgment.

It is assumed that there will be some consistent means of recording potential after final judgments have been made. This can be by a number, signifying the job level of the position identified as the highest the individual can possibly attain, or by naming the position itself. This information would then be entered into the data system used for management development.

Training of Managers

An important part of training managers is good communication from senior management to lower-level managers on what will be expected of them in the assessment of their employees. Training can become a part of a regular management meeting, or it can be done at a special session.

Written guidelines on what qualities to evaluate should be developed and discussed, although they are not likely to replace the manager's own judgment of what is important. Consistency is important, and the ranking process will prevent any one manager from being unrealistically high or low on assessments.

Managers are very capable of making good assessments of potential as long as they put their energy to it and have some guidance. When managers understand that potential assessments are part of their key responsibilities, they will devote energy and time to the process of assessment, and they will enjoy the effort because they will see the value of their contribution.

A key role for HR is to administer and control the assessment process including schedules, instructions, forms, and training of managers. HR must keep its finger on the pulse of the organization to assure senior management that the process is being properly conducted. Although HR should design training in assessment, it is desirable for representatives from senior management to be present during the training session to assure that the management signal is clear and consistent.

Assessment Helps All Employees

Assessment of potential is of value to *all* employees, not just those with the highest potential. The process should stimulate managers to think why someone's potential is low and what can be done to help that employee achieve his or her highest potential.

EXECUTIVE QUALITIES

Corporations that are committed to management development will, almost without exception, develop their own lists of qualities and characteristics to be considered in potential assessment. Although this knowledge can be obtained from textbooks, consultants, or other companies, senior managers will take ownership of characteristics used to evaluate potential if they have developed them for their own organization. Staff input will come from HR, but the list of qualities or characteristics will probably be determined by the executives themselves.

Are the same behavioral and competency characteristics needed for the vice president of marketing as for the corporate controller? How about for the CEO versus a plant manager? Intrinsic characteristics such as integrity, intellectual capacity, judgment, commitment, and interpersonal skills apply to all managers, general or functional. However, some skills and competencies are specific to functions and must be assessed for functional management potential. No one will possess all of the needed competencies and skills early in his or her career, so the early identification of potential will enable the system to develop those skills through career development. A candidate's failure to gain skills and competencies at a satisfactory pace may cause the assessment of his or her potential to be lowered, another reason for the zero-base approach.

To support our belief that the intrinsic characteristics for functional and general management success are similar, we refer to the *Business Week* study of the CEOs of the Business Week 1000 Companies: 25 percent of the companies' CEOs had financial backgrounds, 22 percent had technical backgrounds, and 21 percent came from marketing.[1] Although these backgrounds are quite different, each seems to produce general management executives in abundance.

Most of us have our own views on the desirable qualities of senior managers, and probably our views are reasonably accurate although we may express them differently. Oren Harari and Linda Mukai identified three categories for measuring effective managers:

1. Change agents, externalists, influencers, developers, and revenue enhancers.
2. Innovators, hustlers, and scramblers who are proactive—not reactive—in thought and action.
3. Network builders, team players, boundary-crossers, and resource sharers.[2]

Although these are not the terms traditionally used to describe executive qualities, they are useful to consider in assessing management potential. However, measuring these qualities is difficult, requires work, and requires some skill to evaluate.

Good Judgment

The fundamental tool for evaluating managerial qualities and characteristics is management judgment. The extent of a corporation's success in obtaining good judgments will be in direct proportion to the amount of time and thinking energy managers devote to making judgments. It follows that the key to good assessments is compelling managers to devote time and energy to this most important responsibility. It is not a once-a-year activity, but a continuing process of observation and dialogue. It is testing for those qualities listed by Harari and Mukai (or however they might be listed) through every assignment and project. Based on his experience at Merck, Walt Trosin commented, "The best way to get an assessment of an individual is to see that person perform in a variety of situations . . ."[3] Clearly, making judgments is the most important aspect of the job of a manager at any level.

Don Laidlaw had this to say about how managers should assess potential: "Rather than try to go through and delineate a whole given set of experiences or attributes or characteristics, I'm satisfied that if we train those managers correctly in managing their people, they are going to identify the best people." Laidlaw also said, "You can't wait until someone is halfway through his or her career before being identified as high potential. To me, the first 10 years are the most important time in a person's career from an executive resource standpoint."[4]

Assessing Characteristics

As mentioned above, we encourage each organization to develop its own list of characteristics to be used by managers in assessing potential. Our list includes just 5 categories, but we have seen corporate lists of 20 or more. We offer some measures of these qualities:

Integrity   Managers must have high ethical standards and be honest beyond reproach. No corporation today can afford to put its trust in managers who do not meet the test of integrity. Simple tests of integrity take place continually. For example, an employee gets good marks who:

- **Openly admits mistakes and takes prompt action to correct them.** Conversely, an employee who goes to all means to cover mistakes or to place the blame on others could raise serious questions about his or her integrity.
- **Is always willing to make full and accurate disclosures.** Omission can be a mark of dishonesty to the same extent as giving a misleading or untrue statement.
- **Shows respect for fellow employees.** This demonstrates honesty and openness in very human terms.
- **Avoids the easy road and will perform the hard task if that is in the best interest of the organization.**

Intellectual Capacity   This is broader than IQ or mathematical skills. It includes the ability to comprehend, analyze facts, and learn. Senior executives will not cut it without a substantial amount of smarts. This can be tested through assignments that:

- **Involve analytical and problem-solving ability.** Projects should be assigned that will require speed, accuracy, and understanding of complex analytical problems. Computer skills should be evaluated. Have the employee make presentations that will demonstrate an ability to respond and analyze on his or her feet. Challenge him or her to defend decision with logic.
- **Require creativity.** Such assignments could include development of unit plans, organizing a task force, or writing a presentation. An employee who continually comes up with new ideas and suggestions will get good marks.

- **Demonstrate conceptual thinking ability.** Leading or participating on a task force to solve some special problem or fulfill some special need may identify this ability.
- **Require both written and oral communication.** This can be tested and evaluated daily. Unfortunately, too often there is a tendency to wire around poor communicating skills rather than attempt to improve them.
- **Require mastering of a new job quickly.** This is an often-used and very useful indicator of future potential.
- **Encourage continuous self-education.** An employee's willingness, or lack of willingness, to learn should be observed. Intellectual capacity is reflected in someone who is constantly seeking to learn and understand.

Judgment   Judgment relates to the ability to make the right decisions and having the vision to understand their impact. The success of the corporation may rest on this quality in an executive. An employee demonstrates this quality by:

- **Having a good track record on decisions.** No employee will have a 100 percent success rate on decisions, but the willingness to make a decision and accept risk reflects well on judgment.
- **Having his or her ideas accepted.** This is a measure of how good the decisions are.
- **Making competent and sound appraisals of people.** A supervisor who cannot or is not willing to identify poor performers as well as good performers may demonstrate clouded judgment.

Commitment to the Task   As executives take on more responsibility, their commitment to the task becomes essential. It is not possible for a midlevel or senior manager, or even a first line supervisor, to walk away from a problem because it is 5 o'clock. A manager must be capable of intensely focusing on the job requiring his or her input. Some indications of a commitment to the task are:

- **Showing a results orientation.** This requires being proactive to achieve needed results and an acceptance of accountability.
- **Setting high standards.** Accepting less than the best performance from himself or herself or from others would be an indication of lack of commitment.

- **Producing a high volume of work.** This is usually obvious and easy to evaluate.
- **Using time efficiently.** A highly committed individual will avoid wasting time and organize work with realistic priorities.
- **Being flexible to meet changing needs.** This also demonstrates a results orientation.

Interpersonal Skills Unfortunately, not all senior executives embody this quality, possibly feeling that showing a compassion for others is a sign of weakness. However, a successful manager must get things done through other people. Leadership is strongly related to good interpersonal skills. Even the inherent power of the CEO position does not replace the need for care and understanding in dealing with employees, customers, suppliers, regulatory employees, shareholders, and the media. This quality can be demonstrated by:

- **The ability and willingness to delegate.** Look out for the manager whose desk is piled high but who is afraid to delegate or teach subordinates to handle some of the work.
- **Having the full respect of subordinates.** This requires obtaining feedback from subordinates of the person being evaluated through observation and talking to the employees. Telltale signs that subordinates do not respect their boss may be subtle, but they are there for the careful observer.
- **Supervising a work group and handling a high volume of work and meeting deadlines.** A true measure of a supervisor's interpersonal skills is the total productivity of the work group under his or her responsibility.
- **Getting favorable feedback from other organizations that deal with the individual.** This may be particularly useful in assessing professionals who have no supervisory responsibility. Whatever the job, there is probably some interaction with other work groups, and a phone call to another manager or supervisor may reveal strengths or weaknesses in the professional's interpersonal skills.

This is just a sample listing and grouping of qualities. We recommend that each company develop its own. A different approach to determining executive qualities is to ask CEOs what characteristics they would seek in a potential CEO today. In 1988, *Chief Executive* magazine polled its readers and asked them to rank 10 attributes of would-be successors. The rank order of responses is shown below:

1. Ability to think strategically (tied with Integrity)
2. Integrity
3. Knowledge of the company's business
4. Ability and temperament to delegate authority
5. Ability to generate innovative ideas
6. Good interpersonal skills
7. Energy
8. Readiness to take risks
9. Readiness to put company before everything—including family
10. Ruthlessness[5]

PSYCHOLOGICAL ASSESSMENT

Psychological assessment has been defined as "the application of measurement techniques to understand, describe, and predict work-related skills, abilities, and characteristics in people."[6] Assessment tools include tests, personal inventories, interviews, and simulation exercises, all designed and interpreted by trained psychologists. It is not a new science, but there are new developments and applications. Psychological assessments are used to select for hiring and promotion and to determine executive potential. Its practitioners share information through publications and conferences so that they can improve its application to business needs.

Assessment centers have been used by corporations for many years as a means of observing a candidate's response to specific controlled situations. According to Mary D. Hicks of Personnel Decisions, Inc., "Work exercises and simulations place the participant in a mock organizational environment, thereby eliciting behaviors in circumstances similar to those of the real work setting. . . . Trained observers rate participant behavior across various dimensions of the activities, and then combine the ratings to develop a composite picture."[7] Our definition of the use of assessment centers for assessing executive potential might be: It is a laboratory simulation of decision making under pressure to determine how potential executives would react in real practice.

IDS Financial Services, Inc. believes in the value of assessment centers, which they began using in the early 1970s. During a presentation made to The National Assessment Conference in 1989, Laureen Braaten of IDS reported on IDS's use of assessment and described some of the firm's conclusions:

1. Assessment is not a perfect science—there is error in all measurement. It cannot predict perfectly and should be used as only one piece of any selection system.
2. Once managers use assessment, it is difficult to convince them to give it up. Managers like to have an objective evaluation by a trained professional to confirm their opinions.
3. Because managers already have an opinion on the person before they send the person to assessment, assessors must be direct in reporting the results or risk losing their credibility.
4. HR must take a leadership role for developing after assessment.
5. Assessment can also be used as a crutch for a manager not yet skilled enough or willing to give tough messages.[8]

It is our belief that the use of scientific means to augment or confirm management judgments on employees is sound and to be encouraged as a tool, but not as a replacement for judgment. In using psychological assessment, the focus should be on the individual and how the process can better help the individual prepare for greater responsibility. There should be feedback to the employee in a way that will be of constructive help to that individual.

In our survey of HR executives, we asked them to indicate the tools and techniques used in their firms to assess potential. Below is the percentage of firms using each tool:

Supervisor's/Manager's Judgment	92%
Manager/Employee Ranking	62%
Committee Decision	77%
Written Tests	0
Psychological Assessments/Interviews	15%
Assessment Centers	15%

FEEDBACK TO THE EMPLOYEE

The fact that each employee's potential is assessed will be no secret. Many employees will be involved in the assessment of subordinates and will not only understand the system but will have a very personal interest in outcomes. Here are some guidelines to determine what employees should be told:

1. Employees should not be told how others are being evaluated. Therefore, do not disclose the details of any ranking.
2. Potential has to do with future assignments. There are too many variables for anyone to know whether or not an individual will actually achieve a given potential. Therefore, do not give specific information about future jobs or make promises.
3. Assessments change and what may be true for an employee today may no longer be true tomorrow.
4. Taking care to not disclose specifics, be sure that good employees know that their future with the company is bright.

It is appropriate for a conversation with a good employee to go something like this:

Supervisor:

"Mary, as you know we are very pleased with your performance and the way you have taken over your new assignment. You continue to demonstrate that you have potential to ultimately move into senior management."

Mary:

"What job in senior management? Do you mean that you think that I might be a vice president some day? How long will it take to get there, and what jobs will I get in the meantime?"

Supervisor:

"There are too many unknowns to be able to accurately answer your questions, Mary. Certainly, at this time it is possible to see that you might someday be a contender for marketing vice president, based on the rate of progress you have been showing, and our objective is to help you gain the experience that you will need to continue to grow in the organization. It is too early to identify your next job, but eventually I hope to see you get a headquarters staff assignment where you will have the opportunity to contribute at a higher level as well as gain some multifunctional experience. In the meantime, I believe you are gaining valuable experience where you are and that will help you in your future career."

The object of giving feedback here is to have Mary feel good about her future—that she will continue to grow and contribute—and to feel satisfied that performing well in her current assignment is the best thing she can do for her future.

For an employee with limited potential, the object of giving feedback will be to instill realism and encourage commitment without despair. The supervisor might say:

"Tim, I know you have expressed concern about your future and your belief that you should be moving up in the organization. I consider you to be a valuable contributor and see your value continuing to increase with experience. However, I must be candid in saying that there will be tough competition for the next promotion and the number of opportunities may be limited. I suggest that you and I sit down and discuss what we can do to make your present position more challenging and take advantage of your valued professional experience."

The door has not been closed, nor should it be. Unforeseen events could change the competition and the available opportunities. No manager today has such control of the future as to be able to say that a good employee will not advance. But if advancement does not appear realistic, this should be disclosed as gently as possible.

This true story should illustrate the point.

> Tom was an assistant district manager in a sales district several years after having entered the company as an engineer. Until then, his progress had been rapid and fulfilling. Having spent almost three years as an assistant, feeling that he was fully capable of running his own district, a discussion with his boss had left him shaken. The boss advised Tom that he would never make district manager and that he should consider going back into engineering as a professional. Several weeks later, while Tom was still trying to sort out his options, he was called into the headquarters office and was told of his next assignment as "acting" district manager in another district. Four months later, he was appointed to the position and happily moved his family to the new city.

Of course, you will wonder how could the district manager have possibly told an employee he would never get a job, only to see him appointed to it a few months later. The boss thought that he was being fully candid with Tom. In fact, it had been a very painful discussion for him, but he felt it only fair to tell Tom what he believed to be the truth. But he had made a serious error. He did not have control over the future and the events that would move Tom from a noncontender to district manager. As it happened, a district manager had requested personal leave and was granted the request. This gave management a chance to look at Tom on an "acting" basis. Even though he was not high on the list, some senior managers felt that Tom had the potential and this was an unusual opportunity to find out. When the manager on leave decided to resign, Tom got the job.

If this were a case study for a management course, the class would probably have concluded that the boss should have said something like this:

"Tom, I am pleased with the way you have handled the assistant's job these past three years. You have demonstrated to me that you are ready to take over a district of your own. Unfortunately, the prospects of a district manager's job opening soon are not great and you will have tough competition when that happens. Although I am pleased to have you as my assistant and happy to have you continue in that assignment, you may want to weigh the opportunities of moving up in the sales organization against career opportunities back in the technical side of the business. I would hate to lose you, Tom, but my desire is to see you achieve your highest potential in the company. If you would like, I will talk to the engineering manager to get his views on possible opportunities if you felt you wanted to consider moving into engineering. Let's plan to talk about this again in a few days after you have had a chance to think about it."

In this approach, the boss has not closed the door. He has reinforced the fact that Tom's performance has been good, but it is a lack of opportunity and the competition that may limit Tom's advancement. The boss has indicated that he is taking a personal interest in Tom's career and has given Tom the opportunity to think about his future and to discuss it with the boss again. It will not be the best news that Tom might have hoped for. But it would not be as devastating as being told that the door is closed forever.

It bears repeating that supervisors should not tell someone what will happen in the future when they do not have control over that future. This does not mean that an employee should not be told that chances are slim or that competition is great. But feedback should focus primarily on how the employee can continue to grow without the specifics of next assignments.

To the employee with lesser potential, it may be good to emphasize that assessments are performed annually so that the employee does not feel left out of the competition. To see a promotion go to a peer can be very disappointing. To feel that you were not even in the competition can be devastating. In some ways, discussing potential with the employee is more difficult than the assessment itself. Giving feedback and being candid are important, but not to the point of destruction. And care must be taken to not commit an action beyond the manager's control such as naming specific positions to which the individual may be promoted or assigned.

One final thought. Don't confuse potential with performance. All of our preceding comments are made on the assumption that the employees are good and valued performers. Discussions of performance can be based on specific facts and be designed to bring about improvement as well as to give warning if performance is marginal. Discussions on potential can be less specific and should be designed to make the employee feel good about him- or herself and to feel good about the future.

CHAPTER CHECK LIST

1. Management judgment is the key input for assessing potential.
2. Each corporation should develop its own list of qualities to be considered in assessing potential.
3. Uniform guidelines for assessing potential should be disseminated to all managers.
4. Assessment of potential should be done as a zero-base exercise each year.
5. An assessment system helps all employees, not just those with the highest potential. It assures that all employees are being given consideration.
6. The corporation should clearly communicate its expectations regarding assessments and train managers to do them.
7. Ranking by potential is a useful tool in making thoughtful judgments.
8. Group or ad hoc committee decisions on final rankings produce challenging and defending, which brings out the best thinking.
9. Psychological assessment can be of value, but it should be used only as another tool, not as a replacement for judgment.
10. If psychological assessment is used, feedback should be given to the employee that will assist in personal growth and development.
11. Other employees' potential or rankings should not be disclosed, especially to their peers or subordinates.
12. Feedback should be general with no commitment to specific positions. It is impossible for any manager to commit to future actions over which he or she has no control.

Chapter Ten

MANAGING CAREERS

We would like to preface this chapter with several beliefs:

1. The traditional idea of a career has become a thing of the past.
2. Career development does not necessarily mean a clear path to the top, but a road that moves sideways; and even into other companies, in search of new challenges, personal fulfillment, and growth.
3. The primary contributor to individual growth will be the experience gained on the job.
4. Employees will have a greater responsibility for their own careers than ever before.

The management development process has succeeded, initially, when the employee knows the satisfaction that comes from having been able to use his or her abilities, and to have successfully contributed in the process. But the initial success must be repeated again and again, with added experiences and training, until the individual has achieved a level commensurate with his or her very highest potential. And by level, we do not mean only job level. We mean also the level of the individual's maximum contribution regardless of job grade or position.

To some degree, that development can take place each day, and even each hour of the working day. Daily experiences contribute to individual growth. As it applies to the growth of executive candidates, we will address two aspects of development, the job itself and the career.

REAL JOBS

There is the story of the young marketing professional with an MBA who was moved laterally into headquarters after several stimulating field assignments. Moving to headquarters had been bad enough, but moving without promotion had him quickly dusting off his résumé. However, within several months, his job search had ceased. He was enjoying his job too much to consider leaving, and the reason for his enjoyment was a feeling that he was contributing. His opinions were sought and valued. He was invited to participate in meetings with managers much above his level when it was felt that his expertise and knowledge might be useful. He was held accountable for results. The company had selected the position for the employee's development, to give him specific experience in sales promotion and advertising as well as to give him exposure to senior management. Yet it was not the developmental aspect of the position that excited the employee. It was the feeling of being able to contribute.

A mistake often made before the most recent wave of downsizing was to place high-potential candidates in jobs of high visibility but of little substance. Many of those jobs were either newly created or long-standing vacancies, indicating to the organization that they had little real value and were not needed. "Executive assistant" or "assistant to" positions often put a candidate in almost daily contact with senior executives. For a few months it was an ego-inflating experience for the individual. But then the realization would creep in that a secretary had been performing the work before, and would perform it again (undoubtedly at much lower pay) after the position was vacated. There may have been value in such assignments, of course, particularly in giving senior executives an opportunity, at little risk, to know and observe the work of a high-potential candidate. But these assignments usually fell short in providing real professional growth, and time spent in a position of real contribution would have been far more valuable.

Now that there is reduced loyalty to the company and a greater tendency to job-hop, management must assure that assignments "turn on" their employees or it may lose them. There are three key turn-ons: challenge, contribution, and recognition.

Challenge

Finding challenge in the job is essential to growth and fulfillment. If the challenge is not in the job, the employee, particularly the high-potential employee, may look to outside activities for that fulfillment. Think about this unusual event:

> The plane has leveled off at 13,000 feet, and 20 nervous, but excited men are about to step out of the large open door. Earlier, while on the ground, they

have practiced forming a giant star with their linked bodies and now they will attempt the formation in free fall. After stepping from the plane, two of the men are never able to link up with the formation. Over a minute later, all parachutes have opened and soon the group will be on the ground discussing what had gone wrong. Then it will be off to repack the chutes and board the plane for another try.

When the skydiving maneuver has been successfully completed, there will be no media coverage, no formal recognition, just the satisfaction of having met the challenge. Likewise, within the corporate structure, challenge must be found in the job itself.

Challenge comes from being stretched—being called upon to fully use talents and experience, to dig deep in order to deliver. In *The Plateauing Trap*, Judith M. Bardwick makes this suggestion to management to counteract the effect of plateauing: "Reduce the importance of promotion and increase the value of challenge."[1] That suggestion, in our opinion, has direct application to improving the process of management development. If senior management will put more visible focus on the job content and the challenge that it presents, employees may begin to think less in terms of promotion and focus more on the job itself.

Contribution

When a person says, "I love my job!," it usually means "I am really needed and I am contributing my skills." To the professional or manager, being able to contribute not only generates self-esteem, but also encourages the employee to want to make an even greater contribution.

As far as management development is concerned, any developmental assignment must allow the employee to make a visible contribution. Certainly, challenge and contribution are closely related, and it is unlikely to have one without the other.

Recognition

When I think of how much you have meant to me all these years, it is almost more than I can do sometimes to keep from telling you so.

Vermont husband to his wife[2]

We may chuckle at the old Vermonter, but he reminds us of something that sometimes occurs in the workplace. Some managers have an extremely hard time in praising someone. However, of all the many management tools, probably none is as cost-effective as recognition when timely and sincerely given. Even senior executives like to be, in fact need to be, stroked once in a while, and small praise goes a long way with employees at all levels. If a job is challenging and the incumbent can see his or her contribution, then giving recognition is the final touch in keeping the employee happy with the assignment.

A decade ago, the corporate high flyer was likely to receive recognition through rapid promotion and higher salaries, but that day has passed. Pay is a very tangible and needed form of recognition, but it alone cannot get the desired results. Title should not be overlooked, but unless it accurately reflects the level of responsibility or the job duties, it is a short-lived motivator.

Showing trust and listening are other, very important forms of recognition. They demonstrate management's respect for the individual and the value being placed on the person's ability to contribute.

We cannot overemphasize the importance of the job itself in the process of identifying and developing executive talent. If it is not challenging to the employee, it will not contribute to the employee's development, and worse, the employee is not likely to stay. The message of this era is: *A good employee is a valuable resource that can be easily lost forever if placed in a job that is not personally fulfilling and challenging and that does not offer a genuine opportunity for contribution.* In chapter 11 we will talk more about how to use the job content as a positive tool in management development.

THE CHANGING MODEL FOR DEVELOPING MANAGERS

What is a career? Is it a series of jobs on a path to top management, or is it a series of work experiences that provide for learning, growth, and self-fulfillment? In this day of lean and flat organizations, less movement, and fewer opportunities to promote, it is most likely the latter—a series of work experiences. The development of each individual will be based on work experiences more than on job levels and geographic assignments. Peter

Drucker once said, "You can get Ph.D.'s quickly, but experience takes time."[3]

Any model for developing managers must be built on experience, and attaining experience is no longer as easy as marching through a series of designated positions. Today, most companies have fewer management jobs and less movement through those jobs, thus making it difficult to construct a career model. Contrast this with the boom times of the seventies and early eighties when growth itself created new jobs.

A *Business Week* cover story in December 1990, "Farewell, Fast Track," described how CEO Edgar Woolard's career included 20 jobs in 32 years on his way to the top of DuPont. The article contrasts that kind of career progression with the more limited upward mobility of today's executives and the fewer management jobs available to develop CEOs.[4] Employees also top out earlier. According to Judith Bardwick, the average age at which managers plateau is probably closer to 42 today, versus the 47 in the 1970s.[5]

Further compounding the matter of career development are changes in organization structure. In his article "Do We Still Need to Have Bosses?" Jim Barlow talks about replacing first- and second-line management with self-directed work teams. Barlow quotes a study by the American Productivity and Quality Center that reports that 7 percent of Fortune 500 companies use such teams.[6] (We think this number may understate the efforts being made by organizations to use teams or other forms of autonomous work groups.)

If organizations continue to find ways to use self-directed teams, the implications for management development are significant. It will be more important than ever that managers develop better coaching skills and communications (listening) and problem-solving capabilities. There will be far less emphasis on hierarchy, and far more effort to develop management and leadership skills in *all* employees. Fewer bosses and self-directed work teams will help to guarantee positions for career development where challenge and contribution exist.

Careers are likely to include fewer positions, fewer promotions, and more time in any single assignment. In the 1990s and beyond, individual careers are also more likely to include tours of duty with several companies (although we still recommend that companies build internal systems that encourage employees to stay). If employees are plateauing earlier, the situation is further compounded by more jobs being blocked for longer periods.

We emphasize that the reduction in the number of available positions for management development is *not* a reason to abandon the practice, but in fact more of a reason to have a management development system.

THE CAREER PATH

Although it seems that there are fewer opportunities in today's and future organizations, corporations still need to develop employees to become managers and executives. "Career pathing" is not an exact science, but a planning tool that helps optimize the development of managers. It is probably the most difficult aspect of a management development system because of the number of variables involved, the greatest being the inability to forecast exactly when positions will be available. Yet those responsible for administration of the management development system should have agreed-upon career paths for the development of executives. A career is too short to leave totally to chance—to be decided one step at a time as opportunities become available.

It is highly unlikely that any career will be fulfilled exactly as planned. Yet giving forethought to a career path is an essential part of the planning. Time may be misused without careful planning. There are many variables to be considered:

1. The number of positions available

For example, if the development plan calls for a line management position at the district level, how many districts are there and how many district manager positions can be kept unblocked?

2. Normal retirement age

How much time is available for development and reasonable incumbency in the ultimate job?

3. Number of levels to the CEO

Although the desired career will include lateral moves, the plan must provide for a logical progression through levels, assuming that the job levels truly reflect levels of responsibility.

4. Optimum time in position to provide growth and development

Ten or 15 years ago, a growth business was inclined to leave high-potential managers in one position for as little as 18 months before moving them along. Yet most people would admit that it takes at least two years to really master a position of substantial responsibility, and much of the personal growth occurs only after that point. How often have we said of someone on the fast track, "He was never there long enough to see his mistakes, much less to learn from them." Today, three years would be considered as a minimum for an assignment involving substantial challenge to produce real growth and development for the individual.

5. Optimum number of years required to reach CEO

History can produce examples of individuals who achieved CEO at most any age. Charles Percy did it at Bell and Howell at age 29. Jack Welch was 45 when he took over the helm of General Electric, while Lee Iaccoca was 54 when he stepped in at Chrysler. More recently, Harold Poling of Ford was in his midsixties when he was named CEO.[7]

Certainly, we are not going to hold to any hard and fast rule that the CEO must be developed in x number of years. Still, it would be planning in a vacuum not to have some fix on the amount of time required to develop a candidate to perform at the very highest level in the organization.

6. Needs for testing the individual

We will talk more about testing in chapter 11. However, as an individual moves up in the organization, there are capabilities that must be tested in order to minimize the risk at the next level. A classic example is a financial wizard who moves up in a multinational organization through a series of mostly analytical financial jobs. Once the person has achieved a very high level in the financial function, he or she becomes identified as a candidate for senior-level corporate management. Yet nothing has been learned about the individual's ability to manage either people or a profit center. Careful career planning could have provided the testing at lower levels. Unfortunately, the risks become great to test for these abilities at levels that can greatly alter the success of the corporation.

7. Individual learning (experience) needs

It is difficult and risky to train individuals in interpersonal skills, leadership, managing multifunctions, or relating to outside investors and media when they are at a high (and very exposed) level. There are many basic business and management experiences that should be part of the early growth and development of a senior-level executive.

Developing a Career Path Model

Figure 10.1 shows a generic career path model. It illustrates the complexities of careers and the importance of planning to efficiently use the limited time available in a career, but there are no fixed spans of time for each state of a career or rigid paths. Still, some effort should be made to approximate the time and place for an individual to acquire the desired experiences.

In this model, we assume that a new hire enters at age 23 and that it is desirable to have a CEO prepared in 32 years, by age 55. We show a hierarchical organization with seven layers above entry, each consisting of several salary grades. In this hypothetical corporation we define four stages of career development, each spanning eight years:

1. Learning the grass-roots business

At this stage the primary emphasis is on learning the business with a secondary emphasis on first-level supervision and "people" skills. It is the most critical period for potential assessment, since those who begin to move on a professional advancement route may have difficulty in getting on the management track, although there will be exceptions.

2. Managing operations

During this stage, managers will take on profit center responsibilities and adjust to many business variables. It is a most critical stage for learning business management skills and a critical time for assessment, since determinations will be made on senior-level potential and careers will be adjusted accordingly.

3. Managing line and staff at the corporate level

This stage will involve corporate-level planning and strategies and major line-management decision making. The CEO candidates will be separated from other senior-level candidates.

4. Senior level management—executive VP or COO

Upper–mid-level managers will have topped out and senior-level managers will be limited to probably no more than one promotion.

Plotted on Figure 10.1 is a career path to CEO that provides for two positions in each of the last three stages and three positions in the first stage, a total of nine assignments. We believe these are reasonable incum-

FIGURE 10–1
Career Path Model

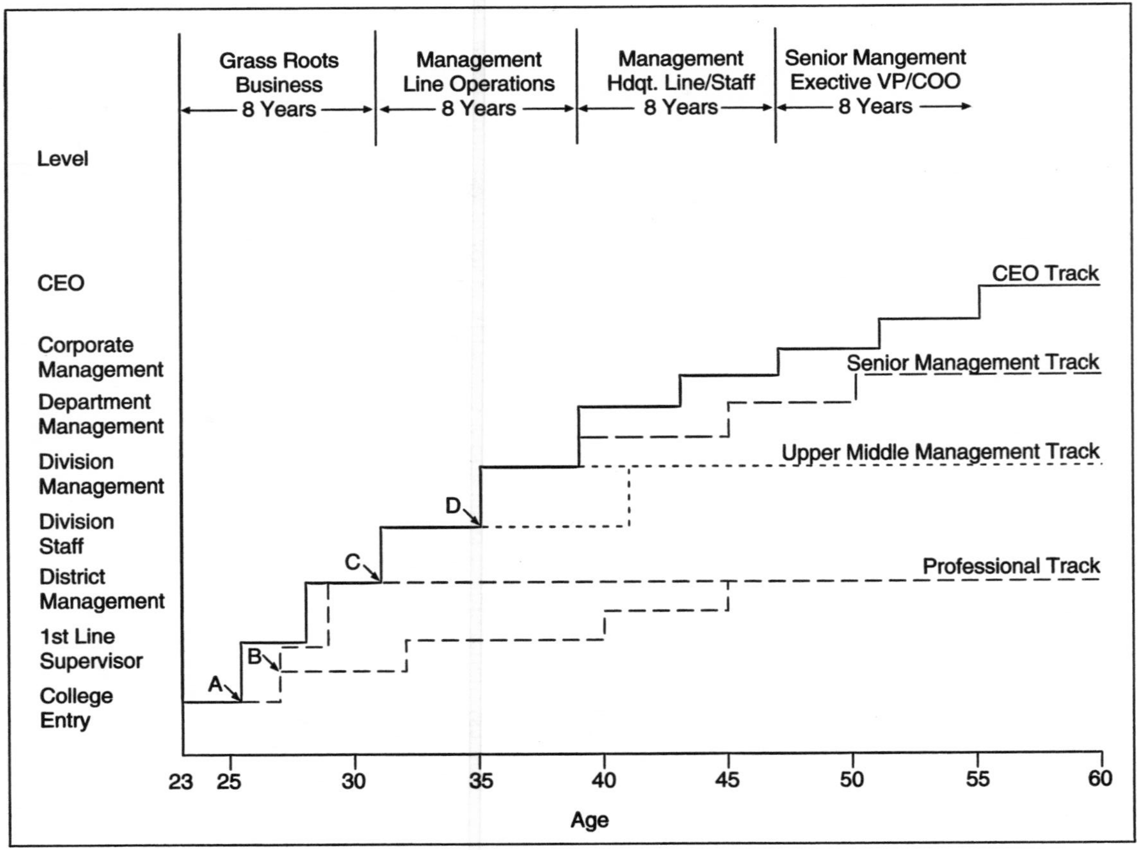

bencies and in general would encourage longer tenure in fewer jobs in keeping with the slower movement and fewer job openings in corporations today.

The model shows three tracks other than the one to CEO: senior management; upper–mid-level management; and professional. Each job change is a decision point for the career. "A" is the first decision that puts a short-service employee on the management track. "B" is a second-chance decision for a late-blooming professional to move onto the management track. "C" is the point where an individual at the district manager level can go back on the professional track, either by choice or as a result of a new assessment. "D" is a decision on whether the candidate still has CEO potential or should move on a slower track to a significant management level, but below CEO. "D" would be a likely point to decide on whether or not an interfunctional experience will be important to the ultimate career.

Even with careful planning, it is difficult to move people through job levels in an orderly way, give them adequate experience in each assignment, and have them ready to be CEO at, say, age 55. Managers who are making decisions on management development should have an understanding of time constraints, and some effort to plot sample careers will lead to better overall decisions. Therefore, we recommend that organizations develop such a model, not so much to plot specific career paths but to gain a fix on developmental stages and the time required for orderly management development.

We offer this word of caution, however. We see management development and potential assessment as a fluid set of circumstances, and we encourage that it be treated that way. Remember that the annual assessment of potential should be zero-base. A career path model should be viewed as a planning tool, not an end in itself.

Certainly there are other ways of planning and charting careers. About 20 years ago, Walter R. Mahler and William Wrightnour lamented in their book that: "Careers are not being managed, directed or programmed. They just happen."[8] Unfortunately, that statement is all too true today, and like Mahler and Wrightnour 20 years ago, we urge that more attention be given to careers before they happen. Incidentally, Mahler and Wrightnour did some pioneer work in analyzing corporate careers and identifying critical crossroads where a change in position requires significant changes in behavior.

A practical use of career modeling is in considering developmental alternatives in the early stages of a career. Figure 10.2 illustrates a working

FIGURE 10–2
Functional Career Path Model

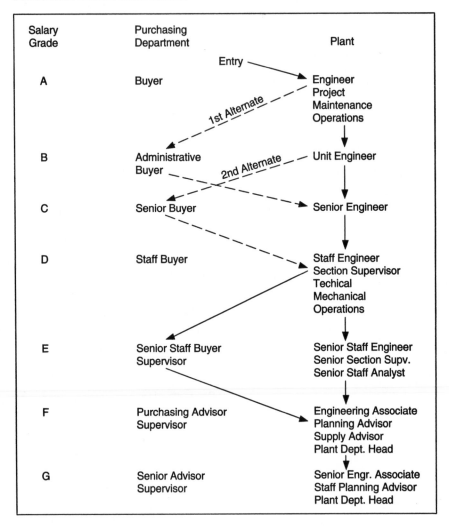

career path model for a function showing positions that can be considered
for each level of development. In this example, the career objective is to
use one assignment in the central purchasing organization to give business
experience to an engineer who is being developed for plant management.
The secondary objective is to have people in purchasing with knowledge
and experience in operations.

Although only three career paths are shown that provide the desired developmental experiences, there could be more. A similar model could be used to chart the path of an engineer hired into purchasing but given some operations experience in the plant.

The fact that there are several positions in some of the salary grades also gives flexibility to the development. For example, if the plan is to move the engineer into purchasing at Grade E, the choice of senior staff buyer or supervisor would depend on the need for supervisory experience. If the engineer had not had supervisory experience up to that point, "supervisor" would be the logical position.

The question might be raised, "But who is going to run the business while all this developing is going on? Will an employee who has never been in purchasing be able to supervise a purchasing unit?" It is obvious that the employee must "bring something to the party" and in this example, that something is the operations knowledge and experience that will enable the employee to add value almost immediately.

The Professional Ladder

The example in Figure 10.2 indicates that a professional ladder (or professional track) exists in purchasing, from buyer at Level A to senior advisor at Level G. It is not an automatic progression, however, and possibly only one or two employees are at the senior advisor level.

Professional expertise of the highest caliber is needed in almost any organization. Creating a professional ladder is a way to recognize talented employees who by desire or aptitude are not destined to become managers. Professional ladders particularly lend themselves to specialized and scientific disciplines. They provide recognition, including salary adjustments, for employees who can contribute at a high level of expertise, and thus they encourage those employees to remain committed and challenged in their work.

A key to a successful professional ladder is to have a higher level of responsibility and expertise go with a higher pay grade. For example, the territory assigned to a professional sales representative should reflect the representative's level of expertise, either in complexity or profitability. Or a senior buyer might be negotiating long-term contracts instead of making commodity purchases. When someone is promoted on the professional ladder, efforts should be made to increase the level of responsibility, even if it is only to require less supervision. It is a fallacy, we believe, to promote employees professionally based on length of service and performance alone, without expecting a higher level of contribution. Promotion should not be considered an entitlement.

Employers might consider putting a quota on higher-level professional positions. For example, only 10 percent of the engineers in a given department or plant can be at x level. This assures that promotions are earned and employees will endeavor to show that their higher level is clearly justified. It also enables management to better control and justify salary costs.

Professional tracks and management tracks should be integrated at lower levels so that late-blooming professionals can still aspire to management. However, at some point the two tracks will diverge. Even then, however, the professional ladder offers an alternative for the manager who fails as a manager, but who possesses valuable skills and experience. It offers a face-saving alternative to dismissing a valuable employee.

Today, with fewer layers of management and less movement in management positions, the professional ladder becomes a valuable tool for management development. The content of the professional jobs can be changed to give increased responsibility and experience as the employee grows, and there will be some opportunity to raise the employee's salary level. Therefore employee development can be continued even when the desired manager assignments are not available. Task forces and project assignments also can be used to develop individuals, and professional job levels can be increased accordingly.

CAREER MANAGEMENT: A SHARED RESPONSIBILITY

A popular elective course in the MBA program at the University of Houston is "Career Planning and Management Development." There is little doubt that students enrolled in that course are more interested in learning about managing their own careers than about what corporations need to do in management development. And this is how it should be. We would never suggest that an employee should fail to look out for number one. Bookstore shelves are loaded with "how to" books on enhancing careers, designed to help employees succeed.

The concept of employee-managed careers may be the wave of the future, and if so, it is a positive change from the days of paternalism, secrecy, and total control of careers by the employer. Still, to have full responsibility for career management requires control over organization, staffing, and decisions involving selection. An individual employee will never hold such power and therefore never fully control his or her career, whether internal or external. Except possibly for the self-employed entrepreneur, a career requires specific opportunities, which will always be in the hands of someone else. Therefore we would temper the expression "employee-managed" to something like "employee participation" or "employee involvement." Certainly, the ultimately goal would be for career management to be a shared responsibility between employee and employer.

To fulfill this shared responsibility we would offer several suggestions, first to the employer and then to the employee.

For the Employer

- Recognize the individuality of each employee to better assess talent and future contribution.

- Use many opportunities to gain employee input on self-assessed strengths and weaknesses and on ambitions and goals. This should come through frequent dialogue. Many supervisors have difficulty in setting time aside for even one annual review, but that is not enough. Talking to an employee about his or her feelings on career outlook can and should occur frequently. After a discussion on an item of business in the supervisor's office, a simple lead-in question might be, "Do you feel that you are growing in this job, Bill?" Showing concern and a willingness to listen will produce some candid and useful thoughts from the employee.

- Require the employee to address career goals and make a self-assessment of strengths and weaknesses in writing on the appraisal form, and set aside time for meaningful discussion of the written comments. Employees will have given much thought to their comments and the comments will be worthy of in-depth discussion and response.

- Provide training to help employees better understand themselves through group exercises and use of instruments such as the Myers-Briggs Type Indicator, which is now several decades old but still widely used in helping individuals to increase the accuracy of their self-perceptions and behavior.[9]

- Provide training for supervisors and managers in understanding of the company's management development system and in how to conduct appraisal discussions in the area of career management.

For the Employee

- Know yourself. If the corporation does not provide the opportunity for self-assessment, and there is not clear understanding of strengths and weaknesses, consider outside testing or assessment. To be a participant in your own career management, it is basic to understand what you uniquely have to offer.

- Be yourself. It is good to set goals and then set out to achieve them, but don't try to appear to be what you are not. If employers really do believe in the value of you as an individual, then show your real self. This doesn't mean display your shortcomings, but it does mean not trying to be somebody else. Several years ago Mark H. McCormack included a gem of a statement about being yourself in *What They Don't Teach You at Harvard Business School:* "If there's ever any confusion over when to play a role and when to be yourself, stick with the latter."[10]

- Know what it is that you enjoy doing and what you do well. A career should be built on those two strengths, yet sometimes in early stages it is difficult to sort out what it is that really makes a job enjoyable. (Enjoyment and performing well usually go hand in hand.) Look back on jobs or work experiences that you have really enjoyed and ask yourself what it was that made them so enjoyable. Once that is identified, let it influence your future discussions on career.

- Take advantage of all opportunities to express your beliefs and feelings about your career. But do it in a positive way, not complaining about overlooked promotions, but engaging instead in constructive dialogue.

- Listen. If you are to take steps to grow and to improve, it is important to understand what the company thinks of you and your future. Only the company can make the opportunity happen, so you must listen to what it has to say before you can share in managing your own career.

- Keep a current résumé and stay abreast of the external job market in your field. We would not have given this advice several years ago, but today it is clear that a career may lead to other employers. The opportunity for dialogue exists with the present employer, but it is more difficult to stay current with the external market. Keep the external market data gathering in perspective, however. Where the present career appears to be fulfilling and to be addressing your own desires and goals, it is not necessary to be continually testing the outside market.

- Focus on being able to fully exercise your talents and abilities rather than on the specific jobs that you aspire to hold. Organizations are likely to continually change, and specific jobs will come and go. A full utilization of your talents in work that you enjoy is far more important than level or title.
- Perform in your given job as best as you know how. In *Unwritten Rules for Your Career: 15 Secrets for Fast Track Success*, George Graen gives this practical advice: "Work to make your boss look good."[11]
- Develop an internal and external network. This can be very much job-related—developing contacts throughout the company and throughout your industry where information and techniques can be shared that will enhance your contribution in your current job. But the network also can give valuable information on organizations and the type of opportunities to which you may aspire. And networks give more people exposure to you and your capabilities. We are not suggesting that the boss be wired around. But we are suggesting that for your career and for the company's management of you as a valuable resource, the more people who know you and what you can do, the better.

We asked Walter Trosin, "How does the management succession planning program relate to career planning in general?" His reply: "First of all, we believe that the individual's career belongs to the individual. In other words, my career is my career, not necessarily Merck's career. It's my career to the extent that my needs converge with or are congruent with the needs of Merck and that's important. We try to provide a number of career paths for individuals, work with individuals, provide them with opportunities to succeed and to proceed up the career ladder, whether in a management position or a technical/scientific specialty."[12]

We agree that the career belongs to the individual. Acceptance of that concept may represent one of the most significant changes in thinking for managers today.

Career Management Is Not without Risk

In 1987 a study by Cherlyn Skromme Granrose and James D. Portwood was published in the *Academy of Management Journal* entitled "Matching Individual Career Plans and Organizational Career Management." Granrose and Portwood said:

Career management programs therefore may or may not generate positive outcomes for organizations and their employees. If programs raise aspirations to unrealistic levels or make employees certain that their personal career plans do not match those of their organization, [perceived] knowledge of organizational career opportunities may force them away from an organization rather than binding them to it.[13]

Participative career management is not an activity to be taken lightly. Careers are extremely important to individuals, and the mishandling of career management could mislead or drive a good employee away, certainly not the desired result. So our advice to corporate management is to tread lightly and carefully as you increase the involvement of employees in career management. And the first step is giving the employee more opportunity to express his or her desires, constraints, self-assessment of strengths and weaknesses, and developmental needs.

INTERFUNCTIONAL MOVES

Even in times of business growth when there were many levels of management, interfunctional moves were difficult to accomplish and required a great amount of corporate discipline, which sometimes didn't exist. When it did, there was what we refer to as the "ticket-punch" mentality in some corporations. Every high-potential candidate had to hold certain key positions on his or her way to the top. Once the candidate had sat behind that desk, even for just a few months, the ticket was punched—the need fulfilled. And if the ticket wasn't punched for having filled one of the designated positions, your career was jeopardized. Two things went wrong: (1) managers worked hard to get their chosen high flyers into those positions, never mind whether the experience would be important to the employees' growth, and (2) because of the rapid turnover in those jobs, they became less meaningful and less challenging. In effect, they missed the development criterion of being real jobs that would challenge and require contribution.

"Ticket punching" did provide employees with the opportunity to learn about the business and get more exposure to senior-level management. But these benefits were marginal when weighed against the negative impact on the rest of the organization. It is probably immaterial to debate the approach today, since most organizations cannot support jobs that are not heavy hitters. And with fewer moves in a career, there just aren't jobs to waste. Each assignment must contribute to the business as well as to the growth of the individual.

When to Use Interfunctional Moves

There are recognized values to interfunctional experiences for those candidates who will move to executive levels. The question is how to achieve them. Some executives seem more eager to accept an outside candidate on information provided by others (usually executive recruiters) than they are to accept someone from their own organization, where there is much firsthand knowledge about the individual.

We offer several observations on moving executive candidates among functions, departments, divisions, and subsidiaries.

1. **The corporate desire to make such moves must be clearly stated by senior management and must be understood by managers throughout the organization.**

Interfunctional moves do cause some pain both to the individual and to the organization. Corporate management must be clear that it wants these sacrifices made.

2. **Only executive candidates with the highest potential and with proven performance should be considered.**

If a high-quality candidate is placed in a new setting and forced to learn the new business while on the job, it is likely that he or she will perform well and before long be receiving the praises and endorsement of the new organization. On the other hand, a lower-quality candidate will not do well and provoke the comment, "I told you so." All too often, managers have used interfunctional moves to unblock a job or place a marginal manager. Such practices, if allowed to continue, will virtually destroy a corporate management development system.

3. **Interfunctional assignments should be used only where there is clear developmental need for the individual *or* there is a specific business need, a less likely case.**

If an individual is clearly judged to have the potential to become a senior executive of a marketing-driven corporation, but has come up through manufacturing, an assignment in marketing (hopefully as early in the career as possible) will be beneficial. But putting a nonmarketer in a key position may not be easily accepted by the marketing employees, although a high-quality candidate should quickly change the level of acceptance.

The business needs, most likely, will occur in staff functions—HR, public affairs, corporate planning, environment—where management has deemed that operations experience is needed. Even so, these fields call for tremendous functional expertise, and there are definite trade-offs to managing them with generalists.

4. **There should be no rigid pattern for the interfunctional moves and no ticket-punch mentality.**

If a job is always to be filled from outside the organization, the unit will wire around the position and make it less of a contributor, thus defeating the developmental objective.

Don't Neglect the Business

Recently, a lower-level manager in a progressive corporation with a commitment to management development complained about frequently breaking in a new boss who didn't know the business. This is a valid complaint and demonstrates that a hard core of competent managers and professionals must often carry an executive who has no experience in that organization.

If the very highest quality people are the ones to be taught a new function, they will quickly master the business and prove their value. In fact, it will be a very valid test of their executive capabilities. But even then, the organization cannot be asked to continually provide training to the inexperienced. There is a common belief that a good manager can quickly master any business, that it is the management ability, not experience in the business, that counts. (Certainly this is the approach taken in choosing many CEOs from the outside.) That belief may be partially correct, but a manager who is inexperienced in the particular business still burdens the rest of the organization.

In this day of leaner organizations, interfunctional moves by executives are difficult to accomplish without adverse impact on the business and on the employees. However, for those few executives who will take over senior management roles, the developmental benefits will offset the disadvantages. Such moves should be very limited in number, carefully orchestrated by the senior management, and of sufficient duration to provide for meaningful experience.

Global Moves

A three-column headline in a January 1992 issue of *The Wall Street Journal* states our message well: AS COSTS OF OVERSEAS ASSIGNMENTS CLIMB, FIRMS SELECT EXPATRIATES MORE CAREFULLY[14] International moves are expensive and complex, and expatriation can be difficult. Still, international experience may be considered invaluable for senior executives of a firm operating worldwide. Without knowing the specific business needs, one cannot say for certain whether an executive should be moved overseas for development. However, if such a move is planned, the same considerations should apply as for any other moves—the job must be challenging (real) where contribution can be expected. The ticket-punch mentality should be avoided.

International assignments usually require the guarantee of return to the home country for employee and family. Thus, repatriation is an added dimension for global moves. In our survey of HR executives, more than one-third of the international company respondents indicated that repatriation from international assignments was a problem. This emphasizes the importance of planning for the return assignment at the time of the initial move.

Not all international developmental moves involve Americans being sent overseas. The development of executives who are foreign nationals is also important to the success of an international business. For example, the establishment of centralized offices to coordinate European operations or sales may involve executive expatriates from different European countries who are required to do business in different countries in which the culture and language are unfamiliar. For companies headquartered in the United States, foreign nationals may have to take on home office assignments if they are to become senior executives in their own countries. These moves, too, are expensive and complex, and planning is required to assure that the development intended will be sound and cost-effective.

CHAPTER CHECK LIST

1. The focus of succession planning and management development activities should be on the individual and on his or her development rather than on filling positions.

2. For a job to accomplish development of an employee, it must be real. The individual must feel challenged and must be able to make a visible contribution.

3. The changing model for management development places more emphasis on the work experience than on job levels.

4. "Career pathing" is still a useful tool for planning. It enables management to establish a broad framework for developmental opportunities, and it gives recognition to the time required to impart certain experiences. However, it must be flexible to meet the changing needs of the business and the individuals.

5. Professional ladders can serve management development by making growth experiences possible when management opportunities are not available. Changing job content for professionals and utilizing professionals on projects and task forces will facilitate growth. It is important that higher levels of responsibility and expected contribution are commensurate with increasing professional job levels.

6. When using specific positions as part of management development, the emphasis should be on the job content and the experiences to be gained.

7. Interfunctional moves still have a place in management development in addition to meeting specific business needs. However, they should have the support of senior management, be used judiciously, and be able to provide a clear developmental benefit. There should be no ticket-punch mentality that a given position is required before an individual can be promoted to a senior level.

8. International moves (for development) should have a clear purpose and should be into jobs that are "real." The return assignments should be planned in advance.

STRATEGIES FOR IMPLEMENTATION

Chapter Eleven

DEVELOPING MANAGERS ON AND OFF THE JOB

... management training or training and development in American industry is a "poor buy," a poor buy in the sense that if the objective of training is to change behavior, most training does not change behavior. And I'm talking primarily of management and professional development.

> Roy Yamahiro, Vice President, Training & Organization Development, Federal Express[1]

INCREDIBLE SUMS ARE BEING SPENT TODAY

According to *Training Magazine*'s 1991 annual survey of employee training, in U.S. organizations with 100 or more employees, a total of $43.2 billion dollars was budgeted for formal training.[2] While this figure was undoubtedly arrived at by sound research methods, the magazine readily admits that the number is an understatement by a substantial margin. By its very design, the survey excludes companies with fewer than 100 employees, of which there are thousands; they, of course, also do a great deal of training. In addition, the survey counts only formal training and development initiatives and doesn't account for the salaries of the employees being trained.

The share of training expenditure for executive education also is large. According to a 1991 *Business Week* special report on executive education, "Of the $12 billion spent annually on all executive development, slightly more than 25 percent goes to the business schools . . . executive education has become the newest B-school boom."[3] But despite the fact that the best-known business schools, along with regional schools, have greatly increased their revenues during the 1980s, there is still some question about what corporations are getting for their investments. John Byrne writes in *Business Week*:

> With all the money they're spending, however, more and more corporations are asking tougher questions about what they get in return. Companies expect that their student-executives will be steeped in leading-edge thinking they can later use to solve the real-life problems confronting U.S. business. What they're often getting instead is classes that offer mere overviews of disciplines such as marketing, taught by narrowly trained academicians. Disenchanted companies are trying new approaches. Many are forging partnerships to design customized programs in conjunction with schools eager to meet their needs. And some have opted to . . . bring more executive development in-house.[4]

As noted in work done by a number of individuals at the Center for Creative Leadership, "Investing in the corporate classroom for management development remains more an act of faith than an empirically justified activity."[5]

The Center's research concludes that formal traditional classroom training for managers and executives is not where the development occurs. A large percentage of executives who have attended CCL's programs indicate that most of their growth experience has occurred on the job.

CCL research over the past 15 years has illustrated key development events in the lives of managers have been as a result of (1) touch assignments (38%); (2) other people (21%); (3) hardships (19%); and (4) course work only (9%).[6]

Our aim in the chapter is to focus on three areas: *specific problems* with management training and development, *guidelines* for making training expenditures cost-effective, and *use of the job itself* as a primary developmental vehicle for managers and executives.

PROBLEMS WITH MANAGEMENT DEVELOPMENT PROGRAMS

The Latest Fad

For decades, training and development has been criticized for being too responsive to fads and not sufficiently oriented to the real needs of the organization. Whether it was sensitivity training or T-groups in the 1950s and 1960s, transcendental meditation or Kepner-Tregoe Problem Solving sessions in the 1970s, outdoor team-building sessions for executives, or TQM, many executives have rightfully questioned why the organization has committed itself to certain training and development programs and strategies.

Quite often, there is not a good answer. More than one program has gotten underway by some person—a senior executive or influential HR person—going off and "getting religion" on the subject. Then, for any of a multitude of reasons, that person decides that the entire organization should likewise benefit from the program. Soon, there are sign-up lists with dozens if not hundreds of individuals going to some training facility to become indoctrinated.

Unrelated to Individual Needs

Management and executive development programs to further the growth of key managers (as well as developmental programs for all employees) should respond to identifiable needs that individuals currently have or will have in the future. The returns on training investments are often vague because the individual's need for such programs was never really very clearly defined.

We are reminded of an earlier experience as corporate trainers in problem solving and decision making for managers from across the country. During the Sunday evening opening session, it was customary to ask participants about their expectations for the week and why they felt they were there. It was often amazing to see how little thought had been given to those questions. Many times, individuals admitted that "they had no idea why they were there." They had simply been told by their bosses that they had been selected, or "it was their turn" and so here they were.

If it is not clear just what problems a program is intended to solve or what skill the training is intended to develop or improve, it is unlikely that the justification or payback for the program will be apparent.

Unrelated to Organizational Needs

It would seem obvious that management development programs should reflect as closely as possible the genuine needs of the organization. However, even during the current era of cost-consciousness, it is surprising to see the kinds of programs that continue to be offered by organizations for which the relevance or contribution is highly questionable.

The "Manager of Managers" Program at Tektronix: In chapter 3, we referred to the "Manager of Managers" program at Tektronix as an example of strategic partnering. Here, we would like to tell more about it as an example of how a program is developed in response to a specific organizational need.

The senior executives of this Oregon-based electronic instrument manufacturer were very pleased with the technical skills of their management staff at virtually all levels. They were not nearly so confident about the general management or leadership skills of middle- and upper-middle management staff. A lengthy multiweek program had been used by the company for several years to try and overcome the shortcomings. The program received varying marks. But after a great deal of assessment work, by both insiders and external consultants, a decision was made to design, develop, and deliver a new mid-management development program. Consider the following examples of how the line management/HR staff design team tried to assure that the program answered real organizational needs and reflected both current and future management skills requirements.

1. The line managers who would sit on the design team would be carefully selected to assure that they correctly reflected both today's and the future management requirements that Tektronix would face in the 1980s and 1990s. Criteria were developed to determine who would qualify to sit on the design team:
   • Executives had to be seen as highly credible across the entire company and especially with senior management
   • The minimum level of responsibility (or grade level) would be business unit general manager (or equivalent), since these independent business unit managers were both the lowest level of general management (profit centers) in the company and were individuals to whom most of the program participants either directly or indirectly reported
   • Executives had to have outstanding business reputations (i.e., reflected integrity in all their interactions with others and seriously questioned the current way of doing things)

- A mixture of managers would be selected, including some who were relatively new to Tektronix (i.e., had been hired to fill openings where internal management/executive talent had not existed). These team members came from such organizations as General Electric, Hewlett-Packard, and IBM. Other long-service and highly respected Tektronix managers were chosen to represent both their current management beliefs and expertise, but also the longer historical view of what was right, given the Tektronix culture

2. This line management design team spent many days working on the Manager of Managers program, involving these kinds of activities:
   - Defining the environment they felt the company would operate in, domestically and internationally
   - Identifying individuals across the entire company who they felt qualified as "good managers and leaders," individuals who in turn would be called on to write "critical incidents" about their successes in the company, achievements that had come about only through great effort and an ability to overcome obstacles (from their stories would be extracted the Key Model Competencies—conceptual, business, interpersonal, and technical and the Outputs around which the program would be designed)
   - Debating (with the assistance of both internal and external consulting staff) the lists of Key Competencies and Key Outputs (results) that were extracted from the stories or critical incidents
   - Identifying selected line executives/managers throughout the company who would be drafted as design team members for the subsequent detailed module development work and, for some, involvement as "visiting faculty" for selected parts of the program

3. The final aspect of the Manager of Managers program that sets it apart from many with which we are familiar, is that before a middle manager attended the first week of the program (consisting of one week per quarter over two years) he or she was required to meet with the respective division general manager/vice president to: (a) obtain a briefing by the GM on why the GM felt the program was important to the participant, and (b) obtain from the GM a briefing on the current business priorities, issues, and opportunities the division faced to determine what a "viable action learning project" might be to work on during the program.

With line management throughout the company involved intimately and continuously in every step of the development, it would be easy to understand that the Manager of Managers program was extremely well received by participants and senior managements in the divisions.

The program achieved precisely those objectives the principal design team and corporate management had hoped it would: an in-depth management training and development experience that was directly aligned with the direction of the company in its current and future environment.

Design Flaws

A final problem with many management training and development programs today, despite the number of resources available, is the actual program design. To look at the many programs being offered publicly or in-house, one might conclude that they were designed for a generic participant. Participants are put through the paces for two, three, or five days, without regard to whether they are active or passive learners or whether they learn best by doing, watching, or thinking.

Happily, the last decade has seen a growing recognition that indeed, people learn differently as adults than they did when obtaining their formal education. High participant involvement and experiential learning designs are much more the norm for both in-house and public programs. A variety of teaching/learning methods are employed, as for example, in the Center for Creative Leadership's "Leadership Development Program." A true learning experience results when you combine the substantial prework for programs like CCL's with excellent instruction, teamwork exercises, and one-on-one time with faculty and other participants.

MANAGEMENT DEVELOPMENT PROGRAM GUIDELINES

The philosophical foundation for management development efforts, whether in-company or public programs, is a strong belief in the concepts of lifelong learning and continuous improvement. (The strong Japanese commitment to these concepts was described in chapter 4.) It provides reason enough for offering a series of development experiences over an entire career, made up of the various concepts, skills, and knowledge components that will be needed in assuming differing and greater responsibilities:

"Of all the slogans kicked around Toyota City, the key one is "kaizen" which means continuous improvement in Japanese. While many companies strive for dramatic breakthroughs, Toyota keeps doing lots of things better and better."[7] Toyota and many other organizations, both Japanese and U.S., have worked hard to incorporate the concept of continuous improvement into all aspects of product design, manufacturing, and distribution.

Many U.S. executives are highly involved in applying this philosophy in their efforts to create and internalize a continuous improvement and lifetime learning mind-set in every employee. Take, for example, Harry Quadracci, founder and CEO of Quad/Graphics, a printing and technology company in Pewaukee, Wisconsin. Quadracci meets with all new employees in orientation classes. During his welcome, he outlines his expectations of the new employees, which include that they will be, figuratively speaking, in the classroom for the rest of their lives while they are at Quad/Graphics. Through this orientation, the CEO underscores his belief in the concept of continuous improvement and lifelong learning.[8]

In his video documentary on Johnsonville Sausage in Johnsonville, Wisconsin, Tom Peters describes one of the core values making up the culture of Johnsonville that CEO Ralph Stayer has instilled in his employees. Peters quotes Stayer's opinion that: "continuous, constant improvement is the way of life around here, with the sky's the limit, and if you quit growing, you're out of here."[9]

Maintain Design Integrity

The quality of the management development program design will determine to a large degree whether individuals gain from their investment of time and other resources. The model below, used by Janice Druian, a management development consultant at Tektronix, reflects the evolution that has occurred in the past decade in the design and development of many management retraining programs:

OLD	NEW
General models	Company models
Theory-based	Linked with business strategy
Activity-focused	Output/results-focused
Trainer/facilitator directed	Diagnostics-based: Self-direction
Manager has a fuzzy role	Manager has a clear role and definite responsibilities
Courses as framework	Competencies as framework

Participants as children	Participants as adults
Classroom delivery	Multiple, varied, experiential learning activities
Treat all participants the same	Optimize diverse learning styles

Develop Sequential Programs

Progressive organizations have taken their cues from leading companies in the field of management development and have attempted to develop a series of management development experiences that include the right content at just the right time in the person's career. IBM and GE, for example, have spent decades perfecting their model of formal training and development experiences, beginning with a "new manager school" to be attended within days or weeks of an individual's appointment to a first managerial position. The sequential programs go all the way up to a three- or four-week internal general manager course. Each sequential program, in its own way, is expected to: broaden overall perspective in the business world; assess and improve skills; increase self-confidence; provide new ideas and concepts; provide forums with peers; and stimulate an environment for continued self-development.

Assure Programs Are Needs-Based

We have emphasized that management development and training programs should be needs-based. The question is how to identify real individual and organizational needs? Organization-wide training needs assessments would be the answer from the contractors and consultants who generate much revenue from such work. In many cases, this may be the right solution, even with its typically high cost. However, ample sources of information may already exist that can be used to identify the organization's needs:

- Performance appraisal documentation

Summary evaluations can be analyzed for a large sample population to provide insights to program developers on some of the critical development needs.

- Employee opinion surveys

When properly conducted, such surveys, along with corporate culture assessments and customer service questionnaires, are typically loaded with objective, quantifiable data that will reveal management development needs.

- Management assessments

Whether completed as prework for extended management development programs (e.g., the Center for Creative Leadership's Professional Development Program and J. Barnum's Experience Compression Laboratory) or used as stand-alone management and leadership assessment tools (e.g., software such as ACUMEN International's PRAXIS or written instruments such as the Center for Creative Leadership's SKILLSCOPE), these assessments can produce great amounts of management development needs data on which to base the program design.

Incorporate Feedback

Good adult-learning program designers reflect a generous amount of feedback to the participant over the course of the development experience. Giving information during the program of how things are going "back home" and how the participant is perceived by his or her subordinates may cause discomfort, but it can be extremely valuable. Some would say that a fundamental rule of change management is pain management. Before changes can occur, the individual must be persuaded that there is a need for improvement.

Include Experiential Components

A very successful movement in management development over the past 15 years (although there are critics) has been the use of outdoor adventure programs such as Outward Bound. Whether for personal confidence building, management or executive team-building, or to illustrate the many concepts of leadership (e.g., trust relationships, risk-taking, communications), this form of learning design has had a dramatic and positive impact on the effectiveness of management development programs.

Focus on the Future

Today, it is vital that management development efforts strongly encourage managers to look beyond the present. Managers need to become more oriented to the global economy and international competition, or simply develop a greater awareness of the demographic shifts underway that translate into the need for valuing diversity.

Whether it is Richard Farson's past work in using computer networks to help senior executives see the larger framework in his School for Management and Strategic Studies, or a decision like Apple CEO John Sculley's to take a sabbatical from the confusion and rush of the Silicon Valley, there are ways and means to help managers and executives get a better sense of the future and to broaden their perspectives. For example, for over 10 years, Farson's program has linked senior executives in ongoing discussions, via a form of E-mail, as they examine a new topic each month for two years. The Aspen and Dartmouth Institutes, through their one-week programs for corporate executives, have helped thousands of individuals step back from the day-to-day rush and reexamine what it's all about.

Work Itself as a Development Tool

Notwithstanding the seminal research in the 1980s by the Peters-Waterman team, the similarly successful works by Warren Bennis and Burt Nanus on the subject of leadership, and the equally well-done research on general managers by John Kotter, it is the work of several individuals associated with the Center for Creative Leadership (CCL) in Greensboro, North Carolina, that has given us the greatest insight on how work experiences contribute to the development of managers and executives. In the early 1980s, individuals associated with CCL began their inquiry into "how organizations create executive bench strength for the future."[10]

The results of this research appear in *The Lessons of Experience—How Successful Executives Develop on the Job*.[11] The book is in a class by itself in terms of how work, the job itself, can be the predominant source of management and executive development. Data was generated from four separate studies, encompassing 191 successful executives from six major corporations who responded to some version of the following questions:

> When you think about your career as a manager, certain events or episodes probably stand out in your mind—things that led to a lasting change in you as a manager. Please identify at least three key events in your career, things that made a difference in the way you manage now.
> What happened?
> What did you learn from it (for better or worse)?[12]

It is the thesis of *The Lessons of Experience* that development during the 10 or 20 years that it takes to grow a general manager depends not just on raw talent but also on the experiences one has and what one does with them. Specifically, not all experiences are created equal. Some experiences simply pack more developmental wallop than others. Further, the lessons taught are not random. Certain things are far more likely to be learned from one kind of experience than another.

Authors McCall, Lombardo, and Morrison suggest that corporations' use of experience to develop executive talent has been a seat-of-the-pants operation. Companies viewed as better managed seem to do more of it than less well managed companies, but our knowledge of how experience develops the manager is primitive at best.[13] The authors also suggest ways a work experience's developmental potential might be assessed; examine the different learning demands that experience can make; suggest ways in which managers can make more of the experiences they have; and suggest how organizations can better use experience as a developmental tool.[14]

The authors conclude:

> But if the impact on the classroom (upon a manager's development) is uncertain, the impact of the on-the-job management development is virtually unexplored. We know the job challenge is crucial to development of managerial abilities, and we know that reputedly better managed firms make extensive use of work experiences for development, but our knowledge of what experiences matter, why they matter, and what people get out of them is skimpy at best.[15]

SELECTING POSITIONS FOR DEVELOPMENT

The Job Itself: Opportunity for Testing and Learning

In chapter 10 we discussed the ticket-punch mentality in which predetermined development requires that a period of time be spent in specific positions. More often than not, this approach is based on history and culture. It is said: "That stop has always been included on the route to the top," or "For one to really understand the peculiar nature of our business, that is a key position to hold."

We can identify some serious flaws in that concept of forcing high-potential candidates to occupy certain key positions. But whether or not the technique is flawed conceptually, it is no longer easily accomplished. In today's flatter, leaner organizations, it is difficult, if not almost impossible, to continue to open up key positions through which to pass high flyers.

In the mid-1980s, Exxon began to consider career developmental needs in terms of the job components, rather than in terms of specific "whole" jobs. Within Exxon, this process has continued to evolve. But for the benefit of those who may be considering this approach for the first time, we will discuss it in its elemental form along with suggestions for implementation.

The first step was to determine the specific developmental needs for an individual who was likely to advance to a senior level. The needs were twofold: (1) to *test* the candidate to assure that the high potential was still realistic, and (2) to provide the candidate with the *experiences* needed for success as an executive. These testing and learning needs were broken into seven categories:

1. Profit center management: Tested the employee's capacity to respond to all of the decision-making responsibilities (financial, operational, and personnel) for a full business. It meant being able to balance all of the decisions that were involved in making a profit.

2. Conceptual thinking: Tested logical thinking, vision, creativity, the ability to communicate in a nonstructured environment, and the ability to start with a clean desk and no routine duties and be able to develop meaningful long-range plans.

3. Supervision of multilevel unit: Tested human and labor relations skills more complex than those required for first-line supervision.

4. Commercial business judgment: Tested judgment and skills involving business decisions affected by external factors, as well as negotiating ability.

5. Governmental and external relations: Tested the ability to represent the company in relationships with government and public.

6. Complex interfunctional coordination: Tested the ability to produce results by coordinating multifunctional activities, quickly grasping and understanding diverse business lines, and influencing actions by staff not under the employee's direct control.

7. Relating to senior management: Tested the ability to interact with and respond to management at a senior level.

Comment: There is no magic to these categories. In Exxon, they represented the composite effort of staff and line management. Therefore, they reflected what the management perceived as "testing/learning" needs and they were "owned" by the line management. It is important in such a program, that the line management participate in determining what the true needs, based on the specific business, are.

The next step was to ask line managers and staff department heads to identify within their own organizations positions that could specifically contribute to development in one or more of the seven testing and learning categories. Not surprisingly, a significant number of positions, not previously considered as important for management development, were identified.

Comment: Again, it is key to have the line (and staff department head) managers themselves participate in identifying these jobs. Not only will line managers take ownership, but they are the real experts as to the real value-added components of the jobs.

The third step was to have each manager, as part of the management development process, identify for each high-potential candidate the testing and learning needs that remained to be accomplished.

Comment: The documentation of needs then becomes a key input to the decisions on individual developmental plans and a vehicle for discussing those plans in the management development review. It adds a new dimension of logic to decision making that may otherwise be based on gut feel or past practice.

We were interested to learn how Exxon USA's program has evolved and how it is being used now. According to Dick Holmberg, Exxon USA's HR executive responsible for the management development program, these same testing and learning needs are an integral part of Exxon's current management development system. Dick pointed out, however, that an eighth category has been added, "International," reflecting the importance of the worldwide needs for executive development. This new category is evaluated in two dimensions: experience (actual assignment in an international affiliate) and exposure (meaning a U.S.-based responsibility for some aspect of international business).[16]

We offer this example of addressing the content of the job itself to illustrate a practical approach that can be taken by any organization that is willing to involve line managers in the management development process. The testing and learning components may differ, but we think this approach can be an invaluable dimension to management development.

Why We Recommend a Closer Look at the Job Itself

1. **It causes managers to focus on the individual and on the work itself.**

Managers will be more aware of the challenge provided by the position and the contribution being made by the employee. Too often, managers can lose touch with what is happening in a position and even think of it only in terms of when they had the job, not recognizing the changes that have taken place.

2. **It is possible to provide development without the extensive relocation of employees.**

Jobs will be identified at the same site that can address the testing and learning needs for the management development program.

3. **The constant flow of high-potential employees through certain jobs is disruptive to the organization.**

It does disrupt a work group to have a high flyer move quickly in and out of the boss's slot. Employees can feel that they are being unfairly treated and are skeptical of a system that seems to disregard continuity and the nature of the work group.

4. **Organizations can become more flexible and possibly move toward self-directed teams.**

Using designated jobs as part of the developmental process tends to preserve a rigid hierarchy. On the other hand, if nonhierarchical jobs can be used for the development of high-potential employees, the organization can be designed to meet the current business needs and remain flexible as business needs change.

Development Through Changing the Job

Perhaps the organization has decided that a high-potential employee, who is a manager in a multilevel unit, should be tested for conceptual ability. The jobs normally considered to address this developmental need—usually planning-type jobs—just aren't available. Yet, it is important not only to test the employee, but also to give him or her some heavy experience in applying conceptual thinking and vision.

Changing the job itself may be the answer. Can the employee be given a special project (e.g., to develop a long-range plan for the unit being supervised or develop several alternatives for the organization and evaluate them against the present organization)? Someone else may have to pick up the manager's load temporarily, but that too, could be a developmental opportunity. If projects are chosen, they must be real, not make-work. (Actually, the manager's boss might be tested for his or her conceptual ability in the identification and selection of a project with potential value.)

A simpler approach may be to just exchange some job duties within two specific positions. It is conceivable that this might meet the developmental needs of two people without relocation or disruption to the organization. Our point is that there are limitless opportunities to provide experiences for the testing and education of employees within the framework of both the organization and the jobs themselves. They may not be obvious, but with some creative examination, they can be found. For example, Sun Microsystems and Apple Computer both have enriched the jobs of their HR managers responsible for the Pacific Rim region by assigning them responsibility for setting up offices in several cities in the Far East.

Also, when job duties are being changed to meet a business or organizational need, thought should be given to the management development needs at the same time. It might be possible to create a testing and learning developmental opportunity. In flatter organizations with less movement, opportunities to fulfill management development needs should not be overlooked.

CHAPTER CHECK LIST

1. U.S. industry is spending incredible sums on management training and development. The challenge is to obtain a return on that investment.

2. The primary problems with many training programs are that they respond only to the latest fad, are not related to individual needs, and are not related to organizational needs.

3. Programs that are designed for the generic participant rather than for the specific needs of individuals are flawed.

4. The concepts of continuous improvement and lifetime learning should be applied to all aspects of employee development with the same fervor as they are to product design, manufacturing, and distribution.

5. The design of the program should focus on business strategy, be results-oriented, be based on competencies, and optimize diverse learning styles.

6. Each sequential training course should build on the same basics of broadening managers' perspectives, improving skills, increasing self-confidence, providing new ideas and concepts, providing a forum for discussion, and stimulating continued self-development.

7. Programs should be based on need, incorporate feedback to the individual manager, and be experience-based.

8. All management development programs should be future-oriented.

9. Work itself can and should be used as a developmental tool.

10. A job can be used as an opportunity both for testing the individual and for providing learning experiences.

11. Any analysis of job content should heavily involve line managers in both determining assignments that will cultivate managerial development and evaluating the testing and learning of the individuals.

Chapter Twelve

DETERMINING NEEDS AND READINESS

A ddressing the future is at the heart of a management development system. The needs to be met do not concern only today's executive staffing, but that staffing that will be required to run the business 5, 10, or 15 years down the road. In chapter 3, we explored how to integrate management development planning with the long-range strategic planning of the business. Since the future is fraught with many unknowns, the planning must be continually updated to take advantage of new information on the status of the workforce and on the course of the business.

The lead times required to develop future managers and executives is long, and there is no question that some sort of quantitative analysis of future staffing requirements should be performed. Planners can become bogged down in a sea of numbers in changing forecasts, but it is possible to develop useful models based on assumptions of attrition, promotion rates, and other variables.

Although this type of analysis may appear valuable in determining future management needs, it is likely to be treated with a yawn rather than with action. Suppose a careful analysis determines that it will be necessary to hire 100 college graduates this year to feed into the pipeline to meet the management needs 15 years from now. But the current business slump dictates that there is need for only 25 new hires this year. Guess how many will be hired!

Our point is that an ongoing quantitative analysis to determine future need can sometimes produce too much information. It is more practical to understand future needs in terms of major changes such as plans to sell off assets, plans to expand, or a decision to build a plant. Then, the analysis can be used to frame solutions such as

- We will need to recruit more engineers this year in anticipation of a shortage of technical managers in five years.

- We will need to train and develop managers for the new plant that will open in three years.
- We will need to assimilate into other operations, 50 percent of the managers in the plant that will be shut down in two years.

The key point is that the integration of strategic business planning and human resource planning should produce judgments as to direction and magnitude rather than piles of statistics.

MEASURING THE EFFECTIVENESS OF MANAGEMENT DEVELOPMENT

If you have eagerly turned to this section expecting answers on how to measure the effectiveness of a management development system, you may find more questions than answers.

Is effectiveness measured by the success of the corporation? Yes and no.

We have exemplified IBM as a corporation that has a model system for management development. Yet as this is being written, press reports reflect that IBM is going through difficult times. There have been two major workforce reductions and strong statements from IBM's CEO indicating that the honeymoon may be over and that there will be restructuring. (Some articles even raise the specter of that unmentionable word in the IBM culture, layoffs. We still believe that IBM's management development system has served it well and that its current problems relate to changes in the competitive marketplace and technology, not to the quality of IBM's management development system. If history should show that wrong strategic decisions have been made, would that prove the management development system ineffective? We think not. No executive will have a 100 percent success rate on decision making, and one bad decision can have major impact. No management development system can produce executives who never make mistakes. What a system should guarantee is that the executive will have had the experience and training needed and be able to draw on personal wisdom in order to maximize the success rate in decision making.

Corporate results must be examined in determining the effectiveness of management development, but even here it is not always easy to directly correlate business results with the effectiveness of a company's management development system.

Is effectiveness measured by the success of individuals? YES!

It is somewhat easier to quantify individuals' success and thus rate the effectiveness of a management development system. How many executives have been developed internally? On how many occasions has the organization had to go outside to fill a key position? What is the success rate in promotions of individuals to high-risk positions? How many midcareer managers have gone on to become successful senior executives in other corporations? (The last question is not all bad. We believe that being a net exporter of executive talent is healthier than being a net importer. We also believe that it is more cost-effective, although admittedly that might be hard to prove.)

One of the best measurements of the effectiveness of a management development system is the attitude of the employees themselves, particularly young professionals and middle managers. Their attitudes will reflect whether or not the system is truly working. Attrition and turnover are not necessarily good measures of this, although a drastic change in attrition may be. A system is probably most effective when it produces candidates who will be sought and welcomed by other firms; therefore, the organization should plan for modest attrition.

Major accounting firms such as Arthur Anderson and Price Waterhouse are highly successful and seem to develop outstanding management. Yet the rate of attrition of quality professionals is high. The implication that if you don't make manager (or partner) by a certain time, you should leave encourages employees to parlay their in-house experience into greater opportunities outside. On the surface, it does not sound very cost-effective to continually train people to work for others and then to recruit replacements. But these firms remain very successful in attracting top-quality recruits. This may be because they offer the perception of opportunities both in and outside the company, they are considered to be well managed, and they remain highly profitable.

EMPLOYEES ARE NOT PAWNS

If employees were pawns on a chess board there would be no need for management to listen to them before deciding on the next move. Usually, the moves would be straight ahead, just one space at a time. The pawns themselves could not suggest moving in a different direction, since the rules are rigid.

Employees are not chess pawns. Yet it is not unusual for senior managers to consider succession planning and management development as one giant chess game, where the rules of movement are set—just one path—and where the employees themselves have no input to the decisions. We have said that the most important ingredient of a successful management development system is the commitment of the CEO and senior management. Or to put it in the negative, lack of commitment is the number one obstacle to a successful program. We submit that obstacle number two would be the *failure to listen to the employees.*

The best management development strategies in the world will fail if the employees do not agree with what it will mean to them as individuals. Some executives have been slow to learn this. They think of today's young professionals and managers as being like they themselves were during the early years of their careers. Then it was "Put your nose to the grindstone, work hard, and you will be justly rewarded." A 60-year-old executive today might say something like this:

> I had confidence in my ability and faith in the management of the company. I earned my way up each step of the way. I didn't need to tell anyone where I wanted to go and no one needed to explain to me what my future would be—I knew what I could do. I didn't need to be coddled! I was never told what my next job would be until the day I was called into the boss's office and told where to report. Some jobs didn't seem to make any sense, but after all, they knew much more about that than I did.
>
> If these young managers and professionals would worry less about where they are going and worry more about getting the job done that we are paying them for, they would get ahead that much faster. Besides, they don't know enough about the plans for this company to suggest where they might fit in. It's my responsibility to know that.

Old-fashioned as that might sound today, there are some bits of truth in those statements. Yes, doing the job at hand is important to future success. Yes, the company knows much more about future business plans and may have a better perspective on how certain assignments will better equip the employee to fulfill his or her highest potential. And yes, if employees are willing to put on the blinders as did our executive when he was 30 years younger, the world would be much simpler for organization decision-makers.

But no, that attitude won't cut it in today's workplace. Employees are like free agents are in professional sports, and it is important that their views and desires be understood. Not only do they have an opinion, but they expect to be heard, and their voice can make a valuable contribution to the planning process.

Here are some desires that employees commonly express and some suggested responses:

I want to be challenged by my job and I want to feel that I am contributing.

In this age of "lean and mean," most jobs are challenging and demanding of contribution. What the corporation can do additionally is to show that it values that contribution. As we have mentioned before, giving recognition is simple, but the most significant recognition comes when the employee's opinion is respected and the employee is allowed to make decisions. In one word, it's "empowerment."

I want to be stretched in my work and to feel that I am growing.

Supervisors should keep in close touch with the job and the employee's contributions. Jobs should be treated as dynamic, subject to changes brought about by the business and by the employee's changing capabilities. In her provocative book, *The Plateauing Trap,* Judith Bardwick uses the expression "content plateauing" to describe a job when there is nothing more to learn, when the challenge is gone. She says that this doesn't have to happen.[1] We agree with her and suggest that companies (supervisors) must continually evaluate jobs and find ways to add new challenge to enable continued employee growth.

I would like to better understand what future opportunities there will be in this organization and what I need to do to better prepare myself.

This is a difficult concern to address, since no one can know for sure what the future opportunities will be and how competitively they will be sought. However, it is a legitimate question and deserves the best answers possible. Although the answers may necessarily be general, there is usually sufficient information for a meaningful dialogue with the employee. Listening to the employee and trying to understand his or her views and desires is as important as giving answers.

I would like help and direction in continuing education.

The first order of response here should be to provide an educational refund policy whereby employees are at least partially reimbursed for outside education courses. Walk through the halls of a business college in a major city at about 8 P.M. some week night. You will see hundreds of people who are making great sacrifices to improve their education—some going to night school for as much as seven years to obtain a graduate degree. The desire is there. Corporations must be supportive, and financial aid is the top need.

I would like to know what the company thinks of me and exactly where I stand.

In chapter 9 we discussed giving feedback to the employee as a part of ongoing assessment. We would emphasize here that time be set aside regularly (at least annually) for this kind of dialogue, that questions be answered honestly, and that the employee be listened to.

I would like to be sure that the company understands some of the problems my family would face on relocation and be able to discuss a potential move before having to make a decision.

Frequent dialogue with the employee is the best way to ensure that supervisors understand family needs and desires. Family constraints can then be understood in the career planning process and in decision making on assignments. Then, there should be no surprises to either party.

I would like the company to know what I see as my strengths and weaknesses.

The key here is to ask! Again, frequent dialogue makes it easy to ask such questions and to obtain candid input. Employees usually are quite accurate in assessing themselves, often more critical of themselves than their managers are of them. A discussion can lead to better utilization as well as steps to improve.

THE ART OF LISTENING

Understanding the collective views of employees is not easy to accomplish, particularly in a large corporation. Unfortunately, the chasm between the senior executives who make policy decisions on management development and the young professional and managerial employees spans age and culture as well as distance and time. Executives tend to see young professionals in their own image, which usually produces erroneous information. Listening to employees can be done in several ways, but no method by itself is totally satisfactory.

1. Talk to employees directly.

Sam Walton, the legendary founder of Wal-Mart, even when past the age of 70, still visited stores to talk to employees and listen to them. Piloting his own Cessna 414 made it possible for him to drop in on stores around the countryside.[2] His questions to employees, according to reports in the business press, were about current business, competition, and often some form of "How is the management here at the store treating you?" Herb Kelleher, CEO of Southwest Airlines, is another executive who has been publicized for his solicitation of employees' viewpoints. There are many CEOs whose management style includes talking to employees at the grass-roots levels. It is management by walking around at its finest, and it enables senior executives to listen to employees. As a tool for employee feedback it can be very effective, depending upon the executive's ability to generate trust and earn respect. And, of course, it is great for employee morale.

Possibly the greatest problem with relying on direct dialogue with em-ployees is that discussions may not be totally candid and that they may represent a poor sampling of overall opinions. Our hierarchical culture still makes it difficult for an employee to go around the usual communication channels and talk to someone at the top. (The employee must still live with his or her immediate boss every day.) A suggestion for the senior executive, therefore, is do it often, do it in different ways (using different questions), and most of all, reflect a genuine interest in what the employee has to say.

2. Meet with employees at meetings and seminars.

Middle managers, and sometimes high-potential professionals, are invited to a corporate or division meeting at which senior executives can meet them, eat with them, and take the opportunity to talk to them. This can occur when senior executives visit a training program and mingle with participants at a reception and dinner.

Senior executives will have done their homework and know who are the high-potential candidates they want to know. Fixed seating arrangements may be used—there is no secret that the middle managers selected to sit at the CEO's table at dinner are not randomly selected. By the same token, the middle manager seated at the corporate medical director's table may have good reason to wonder if his or her future career has taken a turn for the worse.

At Chrysler Corporation, Lee Iacocca holds town hall–style meetings every month or so at which he meets with about 150 employees picked at random. As he describes it, "I just stand up in front of the room and let the people fire away."[3] Such a meeting might not provide specific feedback on management development (although it could), but the CEO's willing-ness to listen and to show respect for employee opinions will leave em-ployees feeling less estranged from senior management. The evolution of "open communications" in many corporations has redefined the traditional view of "who always talks, and who always listens."

Unfortunately, the executive going out into the field or plant to talk to employees does not always listen. He or she is usually briefed in advance on problems likely to be raised and will have prepared answers in advance. By concentrating on giving the answers, the executive may fail to really hear what the employees are saying. Still, such visits or meetings are far better than no communication at all and are well worth the effort.

3. Use surveys.

Carefully developed anonymous surveys can produce a wealth of valuable feedback from employees concerning the management development system as perceived by employees. Surveying is a very valuable "listening" tool. The answers to questions on the quality of leadership, the selection of candidates for filling jobs, perceived opportunities, and needs for training will help senior executives gain a better understanding of employee desires in management development.

If a corporation uses opinion surveys, some questions should address career opportunity and management selection.

The results of one such survey we reviewed were most revealing. There was no management development system in the organization, and the survey had not been designed in any way to obtain opinions on management development. Yet answers to several questions concerning leadership and selection of candidates for jobs indicated quite strongly that a management development system was needed and desired by the employees. The need was being identified even though the words "management development" never appeared.

4. Get feedback through the chain of command.

Asking managers to report on the opinions, desires, and attitudes of employees concerning management development is to be encouraged. Doing so will stimulate more direct dialogue with employees, which is the ultimate in good communications.

The problem with relying exclusively on the chain of command is that much of the information will be filtered as it is passed upward. There will be the tendency to pass along only those opinions that the boss wants to hear. Therefore, relying solely on what is passed back through the chain of command may not produce an accurate reading on employee views.

5. Use interviews and focus group meetings.

Using an outsider to either randomly interview or meet with small groups of professionals and middle managers is an excellent tool if managed properly. The program must be endorsed by the senior management and information gleaned must be treated confidentially as to its source. An outsider's evaluation of the employees' opinions and desires may be most useful, since it will be totally devoid of any corporate bias and it will not be based on prior perceptions.

Our experience in meeting with small groups of about six randomly selected individuals has been good. (To get a representative sampling of opinions, several such meetings should be held.) Generally, employees responded very favorably to the suggestion that management really wants to hear their opinions, and they are usually more comfortable expressing themselves in a small group session.

An outsider should be able to determine quite accurately whether or not the management development system is understood and whether it is being perceived as fair. In addition, the outsider will hear comments on specific needs or failings that have gone unnoticed by management but for which positive action can be taken. Group dynamics seem to encourage more open and candid expressions than one-on-one interviews.

Facilitators of focus group meetings obtain a feel for employee opinion rather than the hard data that typically comes from a survey. The small group meetings are less dramatic, and participants seem to accept that no further response will be given to them, whereas interpreting and communicating survey data is almost mandatory for a survey to work effectively, particularly if it is going to be part of an ongoing strategy rather than a one-time event.

ADDRESSING CULTURE AND HISTORY

Almost everyone has his or her own way of defining "corporate culture." We think that the expression sums up the nature of a business, its history, and the people who have been a part of that history. It reflects the attitudes, beliefs, and values of individuals over time. We also believe that culture is unique to each corporation. It is recognizing that each corporation is different that is key to assessing the needs and readiness of the organization for management development. What is needed for Mobil may not be right for Chevron, even though both are in the same industry.

One of the first questions to ask is, What are the skills most needed at various layers of management given the nature of the business? Does the corporation have a technical, financial, or marketing orientation? Donald E. Petersen, former CEO of Ford Motor Company, said in an interview, "For enterprises like Ford, that have a strong technical base, we simply must encourage people with great technical skills to come into the company, then keep them in the mainstream and get them into principal executive groups."[4]

A CEO of a retailing chain will likely see the need for marketing and business skills, whereas the CEO of a bank will primarily encourage the recruitment and development of employees with accounting and finance skills. (There is clearly a shift today toward a marketing or customer-driven focus for many successful banking executives.) These tendencies are part of the culture and must be considered in addressing management development, and each corporation will naturally reflect different expectations and needs.

The history of a business will have great impact on its readiness for a management development system. Some major oil and international manufacturing companies have been practicing a structured approach to management development for decades, and they now need to adjust their systems to the times. Other corporations have long operated without the slightest hint of a management development system. For these firms, the need is to develop a strategy and plans for implementation, which may take several years.

Corporate leaders—past and present—will also affect the readiness of the organization. A firm that has been largely created by a single entrepreneur may resist any efforts to implement management development as long as that individual and his or her hand-picked executives are in place. The organization may be crying out for a system, but the people in power may not see the need. After all, they have staffed the organization based on their own knowledge and skill, and they may be blinded to the problem of succession. Executives who are products of a system, even from another corporation, will be more likely to encourage establishment of a management development system.

FINDING THE "WARM NEST"

Our basic premise is that a management development system is an important component of any organization. Only the degree of formality and sophistication will change with the size of the organization.

The readiness for implementation of a new management development system must be determined through employee input and an understanding of the corporate culture, history, and leadership. Readiness must also be assessed in each of the various parts of the organization. Because it could take several years to fully implement a system, it is important to start with a unit where success is most likely.

One of the strategies we proposed in chapter 5 for gaining corporate commitment for a management development system was to develop a pilot program in a division or affiliate—the "warm nest." The warm nest will be that part of the corporation in which management has already shown some interest in establishing a management development system. Typically, these managers are the experimenters, the pioneers, the ones open to change. They are usually out in front and receptive to new approaches. The warm nest also may be a unit experiencing "great pain" whether it be from excessive management turnover, too great a need to hire on the outside, or employee discontent. For whatever reason a particular unit becomes the pilot program for management development, it is important that it is the unit's line manager who owns the program and gets credit for its success. If things go well, the manager of the warm nest will become the strongest advocate for management development and will help sell senior management as well as managers of other units on the idea.

CHAPTER CHECK LIST

1. Do business plans take into consideration the needs for staffing at the management and executive levels?

2. Does the look into the future go far enough to provide for the orderly development of managers and executives?

3. Has senior management attempted to find out what professional and managerial employees think about the management development system and assess their desires?

4. Is there some ongoing program or device whereby management can obtain input from the employees?

5. Has the corporate culture and history been examined and recognized in deciding how and where to proceed with implementation of management development?

6. Have the backgrounds of the CEO and executives been assessed in determining the strategies for launching a management development system effort?

7. Has the organization been studied to identify the executive most likely to want to introduce management development and to become the champion for a corporatewide system?

Chapter Thirteen

PUTTING IT ALL TOGETHER

In section I we discussed the changes that have occurred in the business environment during the past decade and how they have influenced the identification and development of executive talent. We also examined the need for corporations to devote energy to the process of management development and succession planning and tried to provide support for our view that the need is greater today than ever before. With the assumption that organizations need a management development system, we discussed how such a system should be integrated into the total corporate strategic planning. Finally, we examined how Japanese corporations practice management development.

In section II we discussed the elements of a management development system and provided some practical advice on each phase of the process. We tried to present specifics, yet encourage organizations to develop their own systems. Section III now attempts to bring the reader up-to-date and to provide understanding and help in how to work with management development today as well as in the future. Throughout the book, we have expressed these beliefs:

- **The primary focus in any management development system should be on the individual.**

If proper planning is directed toward helping the individual reach his or her highest potential, succession plans for filling positions logically follow.

- **The same planning considerations apply to ALL employees, not just to those considered to have executive potential.**

Helping an employee to achieve his or her highest potential applies at all levels. The planning process for executive potential will be better and easier if the same process is applied to all employees.

- **Assessment of potential should be zero-base.**

Each employee should be entitled to a new evaluation annually. Each should feel that he or she has not been excluded from the competition by historical performance and has an ongoing opportunity to demonstrate potential.

- **The CEO must be committed to a functioning management development system.**

A fully functioning management development system requires the involvement of many people throughout the organization—HR staff, line managers, and employees. If the CEO is not committed, it is virtually impossible to pull together all the effort that will be required.

- **Promotion from within should be the accepted process for filling management and executive positions.**

For the system to work, employees must see that opportunities are available. Some circumstances may require hiring from outside, but we should recognize that those exceptions often result from failures in the internal management development system.

- **The management development system for any organization is unique to that organization.**

Each corporation's culture will be different. The people will be different. The existing status of management development and the business needs will not be the same in any two organizations. Therefore, management development activities should be tailored to those unique characteristics.

- **The principles of management development and succession planning can be applied to organizations of any size.**

Employees in small organizations are entitled to the same opportunities to advance and grow as are those in large corporations. Executive talent is needed in all organizations!

- **Work experience is the most important element in the development of an executive.**

There are inherent talents that contribute to executive potential. In addition, education, both before and during employment, can add knowledge and skills. But it is the learning that comes through the variety of experiences during a career that is most important to the ultimate success of an executive.

For the readers who have followed us to this point, logical questions must be, "How do I get started?" and "What can I do to ensure that our management development system will meet our future needs?"

We will address each question separately. We emphasize that the scenarios put forth are illustrations, not firm models, and are taken from the perspective of the senior HR executive.

THE CRITICAL PATH: STARTING A NEW SYSTEM

Step 1: Determine whether there is senior executive commitment.

Did the CEO specifically request action? Did he or she indicate a level of priority or set a schedule for action? If the commitment is there, proceed to Step 3.

Step 2: Obtain CEO commitment.

Chapter 5 discusses eight strategies that might be considered by the HR executive, and certainly there are additional ways of approaching the CEO to obtain commitment. Endorsement is not enough. Until the CEO is fully committed and sets expectations from the organization, the process will probably not be meaningful. It is not always easy to initiate a discussion or send memos or letters to a busy CEO on a subject that will consume more of an already full schedule. But our advice is to take the risk. It is the willingness to influence overall policy that separates HR executives from personnel managers! Several years ago we asked the late Roy Yamahiro to what he attributed his success as an HR executive for Federal Express. He replied, "I put my job on the line every day!"[1] We believe that as a change agent or catalyst, the role of the senior HR person today can hardly be effective with anything less.

Step 3: Draft a policy statement to be reviewed by the CEO.

The written statement becomes the vehicle for promulgating and implementing all aspects of the management development system. Ultimately, it must be in the words of the CEO and the senior management committee (if there is one), but HR can contribute by initiating the draft and assisting with issuing and communicating the statement.

Step 4: Recommend the establishment or identification of a senior management committee for management development and succession planning.

If a senior-level committee already exists, it should be the prime choice because it makes possible the integration of management development and strategic business planning. Then, decisions in both areas will involve the same people. We used the example of how Exxon takes its senior management committee and calls it by a different name (the COED Committee) when it meets on management development issues. For the corporation where there is no functioning management committee, a special committee should be appointed consisting of senior officers with staff provided by HR. It is important that the committee members represent the entire line organization if at all possible. For example, if an oil company consists of functions of exploration, production, refining, and marketing, it would be a mistake not to have all four functions represented on the management development committee.

Step 5: Develop and take to the management development committee a proposal for an annual cycle of reviews.

Here judgment by the committee must come into play as to how big a bite to take in the first and each succeeding year. It will take several years for most organizations to achieve a fully functioning management development system.

Step 6: Develop forms and instructions.

Keep it simple. No doubt, many attempts to launch a succession planning or management development effort have been sunk by the weight of the documentation and red tape. Two basic forms are needed: one to list the positions and candidates for filling them and one to list high-potential candidates and plans for their development. Presumably, HR staff at lower levels in the organization will be involved and can assist line managers in carrying out the instructions.

Step 7: Develop training needs and programs for managers in understanding the procedures as well as in assessing potential.

HR has a substantial role in assisting the managers at all levels in the organization in complying with the requests coming from the management development committee. Initially, a formal training program (probably a day-long session) may be conducted at various locations. But of more importance is the availability of HR to assist managers and respond to their questions. The HR staff responsibility to lower-level managers is just as important as its responsibility to the CEO.

Step 8: Start the process.

Of course, if it is the CEO who initiates the process, it is likely to have a great chance for success.

PILOT PROGRAMS AND PARTIAL IMPLEMENTATION

The above steps are predicated on the corporate desire to initiate the process throughout the entire organization at the same time. However, if senior management is not quite sure of its commitment, the "warm nest" approach (discussed in chapter 12) might be taken. There are always significant advantages to having a line manager become the champion for a management development system, and HR should encourage initiatives taken by the management of any unit or organization.

We do not encourage taking a back-door approach to the CEO. We believe that competent HR management has an obligation to present the needs for management development to the CEO directly. But we also know how difficult it can be to get on the CEO's agenda and recognize that it may be a successful pilot project by a line organization that finally gets the CEO's attention and commitment. Gaining commitment sometimes means that HR must work both ends—approaching the CEO and working at the same time with a line manager who champions the system.

Another approach to partial implementation would be to limit the review to the succession plan for the top-level corporate positions. Initially, the senior-level review would also include only a very top cut of high-potential employees. There is a problem with this approach, however. The focus in management development should be on the people, not positions. Further, the focus should be on the development of *all* people, not just those with the highest potentials. Therefore, this approach of initially working with just the top cut could send a wrong signal to the organization. However, each organization will have to make its own decision on whether to tackle the whole system or work with only a segment. For a longer term, we strongly recommend against an effort that includes succession planning only for a top layer of positions. This approach totally disregards the fact that succession planning at the top depends on the development of people and the staffing of positions at lower levels in the organization. Such planning would be superficial and without foundation.

Creating and implementing a fully viable management development system from ground zero to fully operational takes time, perhaps two years for the system to begin to function at all and as many as four or five to produce significant results. This may seem like a long time, but with patience, commitment, and constant progress, the results will come.

Several years ago we assisted a multihospital health care organization with a grass-roots effort to establish a management development system. At the time, the internal development of hospital administrators was not being considered, and it was a given that each administrator vacancy would involve an outside hire. Since that initial effort, the progress has been continual. The latest report, now almost four years after the initial meetings with the HR executive and the CEO, is that four of the last five administrators appointed have been employees who were promoted from within.

THE CRITICAL PATH: AUDITING A MATURE SYSTEM

No system, no matter how well functioning, should stand without a periodic audit to assure that it is really performing as well as intended, is adjusting to changing needs, and is attuned to the needs of the future. This is particularly true of a management development system where well-oiled review machinery may be masking the failure of that machinery to adequately identify talent and develop people. Again, speaking from the perspective of the senior executive, we suggest several steps to audit an existing management development system.

Step 1: Test and analyze the data.

This should be done proactively by HR, not just at the CEO's request. The purpose of analyzing data is to determine the balance of supply and demand, identify units not producing talent, and evaluate career paths. Examples of data to track for each corporate unit are:

- Number of high-potential employees with department manager or higher potential (for convenience, we will refer to them as HPs)
- Percentage of HPs to the total exempt workforce (or to the total management/professional workforce)
- Number of new HPs added since the last review
- Number of HPs downgraded in potential during year
- Number of HPs who have left the company during the year
- Average age and average service of HPs
- Average number of physical moves per each HP
- Similar statistics for women and minority HPs
- Number of key positions for which internal replacements do not exist

This data can be compared from year to year and from unit to unit, but it is particularly useful to compare over three to five years to get a sense of trends. Sometimes just studying the data will raise some questions or issues for further examination. For example, in one large company, analyzing the data showed that operating divisions were identifying about 1 percent of the total management/professional population as having potential to go to the department-head level. For some staff units, such as legal or human resources, the percentage was as high as 9 percent. This raised some interesting questions. Were more good lawyers going to leave the company because their odds of achieving department manager were so much lower than those of professionals in other departments? Or should the lawyers be moved into operations management and become more likely candidates for senior general management? Or were different standards being applied in identifying potential (the most likely answer)?

The average number of physical relocations or moves may seem like a strange statistic to track, but it is a fair assumption that even the very highest potential candidate is limited by desire and family circumstances to a finite number of moves in a career. So it is important to monitor the number of moves to be sure that they are meaningful and not depleting the corporation's reserves too early in the career.

Step 2: Present the analysis to the management development committee.

Again, the HR executive should do this without waiting to be asked. The purpose of presentation is not to throw out some impressive statistics, but to indicate anomalies and possible problem areas that the committee may want to target in future reviews. The data analysis can be a very useful tool to the management development committee.

Step 3: Listen to the employees.

We discussed the art of listening in chapter 12 and will not repeat that discussion here. However, we emphasize the importance of understanding employees' perceptions of the management development system. Do they feel the system is fair, and if not, why? Do they see internal opportunities as comparable with external opportunities, and if not, why?

Were an outside consultant called in to audit a management development system, he or she would most certainly want to interview managers and professionals to evaluate their opinions and hear their perspectives on the functioning of the system. If HR is doing an internal audit, it should also want some firsthand input from the employees. As we mentioned in chapter 12, if surveys are used to obtain feedback on attitudes, values, culture or whatever, questions should be included that will solicit opinions on management development.

Step 4: Monitor related external activities.

Books, journals, and periodicals provide a wealth of information that affects management development. There has been a great focus on the aspirations and thoughts of college graduates, employed professionals, managers, and executives. Much is being written on executive recruiting as well as the issues involving the advancement of women and minorities. Granted, headlines are often designed to shock or provoke, yet much of the material presents new data to be considered by those responsible for management development. Psychological research continues to uncover new data and alter some traditional conclusions on motivation and leadership.

Benchmarking with the human resource practices of other organizations represents a very valuable way of keeping current. Anytime two or more HR managers with responsibility for management development get together, there will be a worthwhile exchange of experience and information.

GOVERNMENT AND NOT-FOR-PROFIT ORGANIZATIONS

Although most of the examples and discussion throughout this book have involved business corporations, it is not our intent to exclude the millions of government and not-for-profit employees from the opportunities of management development. Our limited experience in both areas would indicate that the need for management development is great, and little is being done to meet that need. Of course, it is dangerous to make such a wide generalization. We know there are government organizations and agencies applying the very latest in human resource planning techniques. And we have already mentioned the not-for-profit hospital organization that has recently launched a successful management development program. But we believe these are the exceptions, not the rule.

We also know that many professional and management employees have chosen a field of public service because of a dedication to serve. Still, we believe they deserve the opportunity to compete in a fair system. We also believe that the need to identify executive talent is just as important in the public sector as it is in business corporations. What can be more important to our society than to have the very best public school administrators, or police chiefs, or heads of welfare agencies?

Similar management and human resource problems and needs undoubtedly exist in both the public and private sectors. The most important difference, to us, is in the approach to the job design itself. In the private sector, each position ultimately must be solely accountable for its contribution to profit. This is a results orientation. In the public sector, a major focus for each position is likely to be its source of funding as well as contribution and results expected. Since we place such importance on the job itself as part of management development, it is important that the focus be on results and contribution expected for all jobs in the public sector.

A second difference between private and public is the staffing of the top positions. In the private sector, the majority of positions are still filled internally, executive recruiting notwithstanding. In the public sector, it is more likely that the top executives will be appointed by elected officials and come from outside the organization. As these are usually political appointments, the top management is less likely to be an integral part of the operation being managed. We marvel at the functioning of the federal government where top executives are appointees, usually without direct experience in the organization they are managing, and where tenure is usually short. Obviously, it takes a cadre of capable, experienced people to keep these organizations functioning while chief executives are learning their organizations and their roles.

The differences between the managing of government and not-for-profit organizations as compared to business corporations will prevail. However, we offer several observations concerning management and professional development:

- **Every principle and technique we have set forth applies equally to the public, not-for-profit, and private sectors.**

The good people working in the public sector and for not-for-profit organizations deserve the same care and respect for their growth and development as do their counterparts in business. If the focus of a management development system is on the people, as we say it should be, we are addressing the same needs in all sectors.

- **Professional development needs are great for public sector and not-for-profit employees providing direct service and care.**

Advancement opportunities are usually limited for teachers, nurses, and social workers. Many, if not most, prefer to remain working closely with students, patients, or clients. That is what they have been trained for and have chosen to do. But meaningful ways must be found to increase the scope and responsibilities of some of those jobs to enable professionals to contribute and be rewarded at a higher level. This is not to say that there are not professional ladders in the public sector. But we believe that all too many are purely based on seniority or educational attainment, with less regard for increased contribution. In addition, there may be assessment and performance measurement problems.

- **Public and not-for-profit organizations should emphasize developing their own executives.**

If promotion from within is right for the private corporations, it is right for all organizations. Why should a police chief or school superintendent or hospital chief executive have to come from another city? Frequently, the reason is not that no one in the organization is qualified, but that no qualified person can be identified. We believe that the management of any organization can and should have a system for continually tracking and identifying employees with executive potential. We also believe that experience is the most important ingredient in the developmental package for an executive, and that through careful planning, an organization can provide those experiences internally.

WHY WE ARE UPBEAT ABOUT THE FUTURE

Some of what we have written may appear to be negative. We have pointed out changes such as loss of loyalty and the apparent influence of short-term rewards on corporate decisions. We have commented on deficiencies in management development efforts, and we have pointed out reasons why they have failed. We have questioned the commitment of CEOs and the occasional narrowness in the thinking of HR staff. Overall, we have raised some serious questions about how executive talent is being identified and developed.

But there is good news with which we would like to conclude this book. No, we are not suggesting that these turbulent times have come to an end. In fact we see change, unrelenting torrents of change, influencing business and industry in this country and throughout the world over the next decade. Organizations will survive and flourish based on the abilities of managers and executives to cope with and adjust to the changing global competition and environment. Identifying and developing the executive talent required to lead and direct successful businesses will be the challenge for many readers of this book. We have talked about the importance of finding challenge in jobs; for practitioners of management development the challenge has never been greater.

There are positive developments in the business environment that indicate a depth of feeling and concern for fundamentals. The healthy substitution of rightsizing for downsizing is giving attention to the importance of and contribution from each and every job. Having an effective and efficient education system is being recognized as a crucial need that is beginning to get attention from leaders in business and society. The early signs of the acceptance of diversity as an asset indicate to us a welcome focus on the value of individuals and the unique contributions they can make.

HR executives and professionals are in a better position to contribute than ever before. The HR function is continually gaining professional strength and earning a higher level of responsibility in corporate decision making. Particularly in the area of planning, HR is making a greater overall contribution.

The change in employee values, we believe, is for the better. Professional and managerial employees no longer can be taken for granted. They will be well prepared, willing, and capable of outstanding contribution, but they will expect trust, fairness, and respect. We believe that this will sharpen corporate management's focus positively on its employees.

And finally, we see a renewed receptivity to the processes we have been discussing in this book. We see a new interest in the necessity of preparing executives who will lead corporations through these turbulent times. The best teams will win, and the best teams will be led by executives who have been well prepared.

For the champions and practitioners of management development, these are exciting times, and the opportunities to contribute to organizational success are now greater than at anytime in the past two decades. It is our sincere hope that you, whether senior executive, HR practitioner, or employee, will be encouraged and stimulated to examine your individual role in the management development process. And following that examination, it is our hope that you will apply your energy and encouragement to help make the systems produce talented leaders and managers for the future.

Appendix

SURVEY OF HUMAN RESOURCE EXECUTIVES

I n an effort to obtain the current thinking of practitioners in management development and succession planning, a comprehensive survey was developed and mailed in September 1991. Survey forms were sent to 170 individuals randomly selected from membership lists of HR executives who had responsibility for succession planning and management development. There was a 10 percent response. Although not all respondents completed the demographic information requested, for those who did, their organizations had an average of 19,000 employees (ranging from 500 to more than 100,000) and average annual sales of $6 billion. About one-third indicated their corporations had a significant number of employees outside the United States.

Four broad areas were covered:

1. Major changes between 1980 and 1991 having to do with the effectiveness of management development
2. Policies and practices used in management development and succession planning
3. Major issues
4. Operational aspects of the management development system

Only 12 percent of the respondents indicated that their organizations did not have a formal management development-succession planning (MD-SP) system.

Comment: The mailing list was probably skewed to corporations with some commitment to human resource planning and thus more likely than average to have a MD-SP system. In addition, HR executives for corporations without a system were not likely to respond. These data notwithstanding, our belief is that of corporations with more than 200 employees, fewer than 25 percent have such a system. Our opinion is based on our consulting experience, informal surveys, and our discussions with individuals in non-Fortune 500 corporations.

MAJOR CHANGES BETWEEN 1980 AND 1991

Respondents whose corporations had a management development system were asked to indicate their satisfaction over the effectiveness, success, or status in their organization of 17 management development issues, using a scale of 1 to 10 (10 being the highest level of satisfaction). A low number would indicate a problem area. Average of the numerical answers were:

Issue	1980	1991
Overall effectiveness of MD system	3.0	6.1
CEO commitment	3.9	7.3
Senior executives product of system	4.4	5.7
MD integrated with strategic plans	2.9	4.9
Employees understand MD system	2.8	4.5
Confidence of employees in system	2.7	4.9
Quality of performance appraisal data	3.8	6.6
Managers willing to accept high-potential employees from other departments	4.5	6.7
Qualified candidates available	4.5	5.4
Key positions filled internally	6.0	6.8
Loyalty of professional employees	7.6	5.5
Loyalty of managers and executives	8.2	6.8
Retention of high potential employees	6.5	7.0
Line management accountability	4.0	6.2
Internal management training	2.8	6.0
Developing through work experience	4.5	6.5
Knowledgeable HR staff support	3.7	7.5
Average response to all issues	4.5	6.1

Comment: On average, substantial improvement has taken place in all areas except for the two issues pertaining to the loyalty of employees and managers. It is significant that loyalty has continued to decline, even in corporations that appear to be successful with overall management development. The challenge remains for corporations to begin to perform in a manner that will accelerate employee loyalty. Despite even monumental efforts, however, it is unlikely that companies will ever approach the level of employee loyalty experienced by corporations a decade or more ago.

The respondents felt good about the ability to retain high-potential employees with some improvement being shown between 1980 and 1991. This implies that organizations are finding ways to communicate to this category of employees a clearer perception of their worth to the corporation. Further, it is a signal that organizations are doing better in providing challenge and growth opportunities for their employees.

A most positive indication from the data is that respondents do see a very significant improvement in the overall effectiveness of their management development systems over the past decade. Obviously, there is still substantial room for improvement. However, to say that traditional management development and succession planning systems no longer work, as critics of such systems say, is not consistent with the responses of these human resources practitioners.

POLICIES AND PRACTICES

Respondents (corporations with a MD system) were asked to indicate yes or no on 25 statements concerning specific policies or practices.

- **46% of the corporations with a MD system had a formal policy, and 31% felt that it was widely communicated to managers, but only 8% felt it was visible to all employees.**

Comment: We believe that a formal policy is vitally important to gaining management commitment. Thus, the indication that less than half have such a policy is disappointing. It suggests that organizations are not doing all that is possible to gain management and employee commitment to their system.

- **46% said that managers are recognized for their management development performance.**

Comment: This also was disappointing. Along with the accountability for management development should come recognition for a job well done.

- **38% saw no significant obstacles to line management support.**

Comment: This low number was not unexpected, but it indicates the continuing challenge, to HR as well as senior management, to obtain the support and involvement of line management.

- **46% said the board was involved and supportive.**

Comment: We believe that the board does have a significant role in assuring that employees are considered as valuable assets and that planning does exist for succession to executive positions and for developing employees with executive talent. We see favorable signs that this involvement is beginning to increase.

- **85% felt that the HR staff were advocates of the system.**

Comment: All respondents were from HR, so this high positive response is to be expected.

- **100% of these HR respondents felt that line management perceived them as capable and credible in dealing with the management development program.**

Comment: As in management assessments (by subordinates), there are surprises. We suspect that an objective audit of HR by line management might produce surprising results for some of these respondents.

- **54% said that their succession plans were computerized.**

Comment: There is still some business left for the succession planning software companies.

- **85% considered that the information was highly guarded and available only to limited management and staff.**

Comment: Our experience would support that managers do respect the need for confidentiality of management development data.

- **69% said that performance appraisals were done annually for each person listed in the system.**

Comment: We were surprised that this was not higher, since the respondents represented firms with management development systems.

- **46% said that performance appraisals were key components of the MD system and heavily relied on for placement decisions.**

Comment: High-potential employees and candidates for promotion certainly will be high performers. Performance appraisals will likely deviate from high only when a candidate is being stretched in a new assignment. Therefore, formally addressing performance numbers in management development is not necessary. Management will be mindful of the need for employees to perform well, even those with high potential.

- **69% said that both performance and potential data are stored in the HR information system.**

Comment: Whether or not management development data is maintained in the HRIS data bank is a management decision. However, because "potential" involves variables beyond the control of the employee (available opportunity and competition), and because systems for assessing potential may not be as formalized as those for appraisals, we suggest caution when entering data in any information system.

- **62% said that succession plans were updated annually.**

Comment: With the changes that take place in the business and in people, it would appear almost essential to update the succession plans at least annually if the management development system is to remain a viable business tool.

- **Employees were informed of their performance rating (92%); potential rating (23%); and likely next assignment (31%).**

Comment: We believe that disclosing potential and information on the next assignment run the risk of having management's opinion, based on today's assumptions, accepted by the employee as fact. However, in this age of full disclosure, we can expect that more employees will want—even demand—this information. Our advice is to keep such information in general terms when disclosing it.

- **85% said that employees have considerable input into decisions regarding their careers.**

Comment: This was surprisingly high and encouraging.

- **Tools and techniques used for assessment of potential**

Supervisor's/manager's judgment	92%
Manager/employee ranking	62%
Committee decision	77%
Written tests	0%

Psychological assessments/interviews   15%
Assessment centers   15%

Comment: The results in the top three categories confirm our belief that there is no substitute for management judgment in assessing potential.

ISSUES OF GREATEST CONCERN

Nineteen issues were listed as representative of some of the challenges being faced by HR executives. Respondents were asked to rate them on a scale of 1 to 10, with 10 representing the greatest level of challenge in the respondent's organization.

Issue	*Average Score*
Inability to project "what the future organization will look like"	5.5
Difficulty in getting senior management attention because of:	
Lack of concern	3.7
Competition for time and attention	5.7
Management doesn't know what to do	4.0
Line management does not see the need	3.8
Inadequate systems (MIS) to deal with paper work	3.5
Lack of internal consulting expertise	2.7
Difficulty in making interfunctional transfers because of	3.9
Compensation package	2.6
Resistance to relocation	4.6
Spouse's job (relocation)	4.6
Adequately identifying potential	5.5
Record of high success in promotion to key positions	4.8
Removing nonperformers to free up key positions	5.5
Locating qualified women and minorities—	
As new, college hires	6.1
Outside, experienced hires for key positions	6.6
Internal candidates for key positions	7.2
Obtaining appropriate international experience for key employees (international corporations only)	4.5
Repatriation to the home country (international corporations only)	4.2

Comment: Issues related to locating qualified women and minorities ranked first, second, and third. This indicates that the respondents feel that their companies are not moving as fast as they should in the advancement of women and minorities.

The next issue of great concern was the difficulty in getting senior management's attention because of the competition from other business matters. Respondents did not feel that the problem was lack of concern for management development, but that there wasn't enough time to devote to it. To us, this answer indicates that the commitment was not really there. If it were, we believe the senior management would set different priorities.

Three issues tie for fifth place—the inability to project what the future organization will look like, adequately identifying potential, and removing nonperformers to free up key positions. The inability to project into the future points up the need for integration of strategic and management development planning, the subject of the chapter 3.

The problem of blocked key jobs does not necessarily indicate poor performance, however. It indicates that a good performing incumbent may not be promotable and have no place else to go. Our experience indicates that there always will be a significant number of key jobs that are blocked. The challenge is to find ways to creatively unblock as many positions as possible by identifying meaningful assignments for incumbents and selecting candidates who will have the potential to be promoted. The high level of concern over this issue leads us to believe that the respondents are deeply involved with a viable management development system.

It is no surprise to us that identifying high potential is a major concern. It is not an exact science and requires thoughtful judgments. Practitioners continue to search for new tools to make potential assessment more accurate.

OPERATIONAL ASPECTS OF THE SYSTEM

Twelve questions were asked concerning the operation of the management development system. The variety of answers does not lend itself to a statistical analysis, but the nature of the responses along with our comments are shown below.

- **The vast majority of companies have annual management development reviews.**

Comment: This indicates that the annual review is the heart of a management development system.

- **The vast majority have a standing corporate review committee, consisting of four to eight members. The committees meet on average twice a year.**

Comment: This suggests a less than desired commitment. Although the formal review for any one department may be annual, we believe there should be reviews of several departments plus other management development decisions and issues to be discussed throughout the year.

- **The highest level review will consider, on average, more than 100 total positions although the responses varied from a few positions to several hundred. The vast majority of companies hold management development reviews at three or more organizational levels.**

Comment: This question may have been poorly stated. If the responses are intended to mean that separate reviews were held at several different levels, a high level of commitment is indicated and this is good news. However, some respondents may have meant only that several organizational levels were reviewed in the senior-level review.

- **The typical agenda for the vast majority of reviews includes discussion of: organization; succession plans for key positions; individual development plans for incumbents; and a list of high potential candidates and plans.**

Comment: Including discussion of organization in management development reviews is not only appropriate but helps in integrating the MD planning with strategic business planning.

- **About two-thirds of the companies include separate discussions on women and minorities.**

Comment: We believe that requiring a separate discussion of the management development of women and minorities during the annual MD review gains commitment and accountability of the line management.

- **About two-thirds also discuss related topics such as recruitment, management training, attrition, and compensation issues.**

  Comment: As with women and minorities, asking questions on related issues indicates senior management's interest and requires an accountability for management development that is much broader than names and charts. We encourage adding these items to the review agenda.

- **Only one-third addresses macro supply/demand forecasts for human resources.**

  Comment: Normally these forecasts are the responsibility of HR and/or a corporate or strategic planning group. It is not necessary, to spend time addressing them during the MD review.

- **Most succession plans are made for three or more years forward and show three or more candidates for each key position.**

  Comment: We believe that planning for three years ahead is the practical time frame in view of the rapidly changing business needs in many companies today.

- **Individual development plans are usually for two years forward.**

  Comment: We recommend planning for five years ahead, or the next two assignments. It will be hard to hold to very specific plans for individuals, but general plans should be considered over the next two assignments.

- **All but one of the companies has a job posting system, but most do not post key management and executive positions.**

  Comment: Job posting for key management and executive positions could be disruptive—a topic for water cooler discussions—and serve no real purpose, since the decisions will be made by senior management. Employee input should come through normal review and counseling sessions. Employees should not be asked to apply for very senior management positions.

- **Most companies interview internal management candidates for key management positions before a final decision is made.**

  Comment: An interview can and often does produce excellent information, but it may not be necessary if the management development system is current and includes current management judgments.

WHAT IS THE NUMBER ONE CHALLENGE?

Finally, we asked for a narrative response to this statement.

Please state what you consider to be the number one "challenge" you face in the next three years as the person responsible for your organization's management development and succession planning program.

The responses were thoughtful, varied, and interesting:

- Fairly removing individuals who are in good development jobs and blocking opportunities for others with potential
- Getting top management to recognize the importance of spending the time to develop a world-class effort
- To cope with the growth rate envisaged in terms of acquiring the human resources with the right "mixture" of "mind" and "managerial" ability
- Correctly predicting organization growth and related HR needs and meeting these needs internally as much as possible
- Keeping up interest level and momentum
- Assuring [current succession] plans are consulted before appointments are made
- Better automation to broaden access and reduce paperwork
- Better integration with business plans
- Development of leadership skills and identification of potential leaders (versus managers)
- Talent assessment; potential and development needs matched with the individual development plans . . . and then execute
- To gain broad-based support throughout the executive management staff
- To have adequate human resources systems capability for tracking purposes
- To take successful elements of the program further down into the organization
- Furthering ownership by line managers of this process as a tool for them as well as corporate

- Getting all members of senior management to participate in the process
- Performance appraisal
- More "years forward"—longer term focus

The survey responses were very useful to us in preparing this book, and we have tried to address many of the issues raised. To those who took the time to respond, we thank you.

Notes

Introduction

1. C. Handy, *The Age of Unreason* (Boston: Harvard Business School Press, 1990), p. 6. Copyright 1989 by Charles Handy.

Chapter 1: The New Era

1. A. Toffler, *Future Shock* (New York: Random House, 1970), p. 11.
2. A. Deutschman, "What 25 Year Olds Want," *Fortune*, August 27, 1990, p. 42.
3. R. M. Tomasko, *Downsizing: Reshaping the Corporation of the Future* (New York: AMACON, 1987), pp. 1–2.
4. *The Wall Street Journal*, December 20, 1990, p. A-8.
5. B. Burrough and J. Helyar, *Barbarians at the Gate: The Fall of RJR Nabisco* (New York: Harper Perennial, 1991).

Chapter 2: Internal Management Development

1. *Fortune*, Apr. 8, 1991, p. 12.
2. R. M. Tomasko, *"Downsizing: Reshaping the Corporation for the Future,"* (New York: AMACON, 1987) p. 28.
3. A. B. Fisher, "Morale Crisis," *Fortune*, Nov. 18, 1991, p. 70.
4. R. Levering, *A Great Place to Work*, (New York: Random House, 1988), p. 210.
5. Levering, p. 210.
6. T. Boone Pickens, Jr., *Boone* (Boston: Houghton Mifflin, 1987), pp. 136–137.
7. Pickens, p. 147.

8. W. Edwards Deming, quoted in *The Wall Street Journal*, June 4, 1990, p. 39.
9. M. W. McCall, Jr., M. M. Lombardo, A. M. Morrison, "Trial By Fire: Learning from Job Assignments." In *The Lessons of Experience: How Successful Executives Develop on the Job*, (Lexington, Mass.: Lexington Books, 1988), pp. 16–18.
10. Charles Cawley, speech to the National Quality Forum, New York, Oct. 3, 1989.
11. G. F. Will, *Men at Work: The Craft of Baseball* (New York: McMillan, 1990), p. 2.
12. Will, p. 63.

Chapter 3: Integration with Strategic Business Planning

1. Some of these corporate culture writers include: S. M. Davis, *Managing Corporate Culture* (Cambridge, Mass.: Ballinger, 1984); E. H. Schein, *Organizational Culture and Leadership* (San Francisco: Jossey-Bass, 1985); L. G. Bolman and T. E. Deal, *Modern Approaches to Understanding and Managing Organizations* (San Francisco: Jossey-Bass, 1984); R. H. Kilman et al., *Gaining Control of the Corporate Culture*, (San Francisco: Jossey-Bass, 1985).
2. T. J. Watson, Jr., "A Business and Its Beliefs: The Ideas that Helped Build IBM," McKinsey Foundation Lecture Series (New York: McGraw Hill, 1963), p. 5. Reproduced with permission of McGraw-Hill, Inc.
3. S. M. Davis, *Managing Corporate Culture* (Cambridge, Mass.: Ballinger, 1984), p. 7.
4. R. Howard, "Values Make the Company—An Interview With Robert Haas" *Harvard Business Review*, Sept./Oct. 1990, p. 133.
5. Steve McMahon, personal interview.
6. Eric Vetter, personal interview.
7. McMahon, personal interview.
8. Bill Rhoades, personal interview.
9. Vetter, personal interview.
10. J. A. Byrne, "Back to School: A Special Report on Executive Education" *Business Week*, Oct. 28, 1991, p. 103.
11. J. K. Berry, "Linking Management Development to Business Strategies," *Training and Development Journal*, Aug. 1990, p. 21.

Chapter 4: Lessons from Japan

1. "Japan Jabs U.S. Business—Again," *The Houston Post*, Jan. 26, 1992, p. A-1.
2. *The Houston Post*, Jan. 26, 1992, p. A-1.
3. C. V. Prestowitz, Jr., *Trading Places* (New York: Basic Books, 1989), p. 289.
4. J. J. Fucini and S. Fucini, *Working for the Japanese* (New York: The Free Press, 1990), p. 7.
5. C. J. Grayson, Jr. and C. O'Dell, *American Business: A Two-Minute Warning* (New York: The Free Press, 1988), p. 198.
6. R. L. Shook, *Honda: An American Success Story* (New York: Prentice Hall, 1988), p. 167.
7. Shook, p. 169.
8. Fucini, p. 50–55.
9. Fucini, p. 56.
10. Grayson, p. 268.
11. Grayson, p. 273.
12. R. L. Tung, *Key to Japan's Economic Strength: Human Power* (Lexington, Mass: D. C. Heath, 1984), p. 182.
13. *Parade Magazine*, Aug. 25, 1991, p. 3.
14. Shook, p. 97.
15. M. K. Starr, "From Tokyo to Tennessee," *Chief Executive*, March 1990, p. 45.
16. Grayson, p. 197.
17. Grayson, pp. 196–197.
18. Grayson, p. 314.
19. Prestowitz, p. 290.
20. W. G. Ouchi, *Theory Z* (New York: Avon, 1982), p. 22.
21. J. Kotkin and Y. Kishimoto, *The Third Century: America's Resurgence in the Asian Era*, (New York: Crown, 1988), p. 136.
22. I. Hockaday, "How Hallmark Goes about Being Low-Cost Producer," *Fortune*, May 25, 1987, p. 31.
23. A. Morita and S. Ishihara, quoted in "The Japan That Can Say No," *Management Review*, Aug. 1990, p. 7.
24. "Bank of Tokyo Exec Debunks Japanese Stereotypes," *Management Review*, Aug. 1990, p. 7.
25. Tung, p. 42.
26. Kotkin, p. 136.

27. Kotkin, p. 136.
28. T. R. Horton, "The Pacific Rim: Threat or Opportunity," *Management Review*, Aug. 1990, p. 6.
29. Business Week/NHK/Harris Poll, *Business Week*, Sept. 3, 1990, p. 49.
30. J. C. McCune, "Japan Says Sayonara to Womb-to-Tomb Management," *Management Review*, Nov. 1990, p. 13.
31. J. E. Rehfeld, "What Working for a Japanese Company Taught Me" *Harvard Business Review*, Nov./Dec. 1990, p. 173.
32. Ouchi, p. 78.
33. Rehfeld, p. 50.
34. Fucini, p. 223.

Chapter 5: The Critical Need for Corporate Commitment

1. Eric Vetter, personal interview.
2. Walter R. Trosin, personal interview.
3. B. Burlingham and C. Hartman, "Cowboy Capitalist," *INC. Magazine*, Jan. 1989, p. 66.
4. J. Kotter, *The Leadership Factor* (New York: The Free Press, 1988), pp. 100–101.
5. R. Levering, *A Great Place to Work*) New York: Random House, 1988), p. 213.
6. H. M. Larson, E. H. Knowlton, and C. S. Popple, *New Horizons: History of Standard Oil Company (New Jersey)* (New York: Harper and Row, 1971), pp. 593–96.
7. Exxon Corporation Proxy Statement, March 7, 1991. Average company service of Messrs. Clarke, McIvor, Rawl, Raymond, and Sitter.
8. Don Laidlaw, personal interview.
9. Trosin, personal interview.
10. W. H. Mahler and F. Gaines, Jr., *Succession Planning in Leading Companies* (Midland Park, NJ: Mahler, 1983), p. 9.
11. "Caught in the Middle: Six Managers Speak Out on Corporate Life," *Business Week*, Sept. 12, 1988, p. 82.

Chapter 6: Making the System Work

1. Eric Vetter, personal interview.
2. Francis J. Aguilar and Richard G. Hamermesh, General Electric: John F. Welch, Jr., Chairman of the Board, Video, 9-882-524. (Boston: Harvard Business School, 1982).
3. Rosabeth Moss Kanter and Paul F. Myers, Banc One Corporation—1989, Case 9-390-029. (Boston: Harvard Business School, 1989, p. 1).
4. P. Sellers, "Does the CEO Really Matter?" *Fortune*, Apr. 22, 1991, p. 80.
5. Sellers, p. 90.
6. Walter R. Trosin, personal interview.
7. Steve McMahon, personal interview.
8. Richard F. Vancil, General Electric Co.: Management Succession and a New Staff Role, Video, 9-882-554. (Boston: Harvard Business School, 1982).
9. T. R. Horton, "The Anomoly of Corporate Boards," *Management Review*, August 1990, p. 4.
10. Wall Street Journal, June 6, 1991, p. 1.
11. Houston Chronicle, Oct. 24,1991, p. 1.
12. Houston Chronicle, Oct. 26, 1991, p. 1A.
13. *Business Week*, Nov. 4, 1991, p. 134.
14. Judith M. Bardwick, *Danger in the Comfort Zone: From Boardroom to Mailroom—How to Break the Entitlement Habit That's Killing American Business* (New York: AMACON, 1991), p. 14.
15. Thomas R. Horton and Peter C. Reid, *Beyond the Trust Gap—Forging a New Partnership Between Managers and Their Employees* (Homewood, Ill.: Business One Irwin, 1991).

Chapter 7: Review and Stewardship

1. Don Laidlaw, personal interview.
2. Eric Vetter, personal interview.
3. Ibid.
4. T. Peters, *Thriving on Chaos* (New York: Harper & Row, 1987), p. 524.
5. Steve McMahon, personal interview.
6. Walter R. Trosin, personal interview.

7. Richard L. Holmberg, personal interview.
8. "HR for HR at ARCO," *HR REPORTER*, Sept. 1990, p. 7.
9. P. F. Drucker, *Management Tasks, Responsibilities, Practices* (New York: Harper & Row, 1973), p. xi.
10. Trosin, personal interview.
11. McMahon, personal interview.

Chapter 8: Addressing Diversity

1. R. Thomas, Jr., "Beyond Race and Gender," (New York: AMACON, 1991), p. ix.
2. Newsletter from Office of the Dean, College of Engineering, Cornell University, Dec. 1991.
3. "Throwing Stones at Glass Ceilings," *Business Week*, Aug. 19, 1991, p. 29.
4. "Race in the Workplace: Is Affirmative Action Really Working?" *Business Week*, July 8, 1991, p. 63.
5. *Business Week*, July 8, 1991, p. 53.
6. *Houston Chronicle*, Aug. 9, 1991, Source: U.S. Department of Labor.
7. *Kiplinger Washington Letter*, June 21, 1991. Source: Urban Institute (The non-white population in the United States, including Hispanics, will increase from 25 to 40 percent over the next 50 years.) W. R. Johnston and A. H. Packer, *Workforce 2000: Work and Workers for the 21st Century* (Hudson Institute, 1987), p. xxi (85 percent of the net new additions to the workforce between 1985 and 2000 will be women and minorities).
8. G. Putka, *The Wall Street Journal*, "Concern Goes Up As SAT Scores Go Down," Aug. 27, 1991.
9. *The Houston Post*, Aug. 29, 1991, Source: Houston Independent School District.
10. J. J. Oxford, *Time*, "Are Black Colleges Worth Saving?" Nov. 11, 1991, p. 81.
11. *The MacNeil/Lehrer News Hour*, Nov. 12, 1991.
12. "The New Facts of Life," *Harvard Business Review* Jan.-Feb. 1989, p. 70.
13. "Meet DuPont's In-House Conscience," *Business Week*, June 24, 1991, p. 62.
14. S. Shellenbarger, "More Job Seekers Put Family Needs First," *The Wall Street Journal*, Nov. 15, 1991, p. B1.

15. K. Cramer and J. Pearce, "Work and Family Policies Become Family Tools," *Management Review*, Nov. 1990, p. 42.
16. "Letters to the Editor," *Harvard Business Review*, June-July 1990, p. 194.
17. A. Deutschman, "Pioneers of the New Balance," *Fortune*, May 20, 1990, p. 60.
18. "The New Facts of Life," *Harvard Business Review*, Jan.-Feb. 1989.
19. *Harvard Business Review*, Jan.-Feb. 1989.
20. R. R. Thomas, Jr., "Beyond the Limits of Affirmative Action," *HR Magazine*, June 1990, p. 208.
21. *The MacNeil/Lehrer News Hour*, Nov. 12, 1991.
22. J. Castro, "Get Set: Here They Come!", *Time*, Fall, 1990 (special edition), p. 51.
23. M. Loden and J. B. Rosener, *Workforce America! Managing Employee Diversity as a Vital Resource* (Homewood, Ill.: Business One Irwin, 1991).

Chapter 9: Assessing Potential

1. *Business Week*, Nov. 25, 1991, p. 180.
2. *Management Review*, Aug. 1990, p. 20.
3. Walter R. Trosin, personal interview.
4. Don Laidlaw, personal interview.
5. "How CEOs Plan for Succession," *Chief Executive*, May-June 1988, p. 64.
6. "What Do Assessors Do, and Why Do We Need Them?" Proceedings from The 1989 National Assessment Conference October 1–3, 1989, p. 48. Co-sponsored by Personnel Decisions, Inc. and the Department of Psychology, University of Minnesota.
7. Ibid.
8. "Can Assessment Add Value to the Selection and Development of Sales Manager?", Proceedings from The National Assessment Conference, pp. 20, 21.

Notes   Chapter 10: Managing Careers

1. J. M. Bardwick, *The Plateauing Trap* (New York: Bantam, 1988) p. 131.
2. *Forbes*, Nov. 26, 1990, p. 320.

3. Peter Drucker, *Forbes*, Aug. 19, 1991, p. 72.
4. *Business Week*, Dec. 10, 1990, p. 192.
5. Bardwick, p. 45.
6. *Houston Chronicle*, Nov. 12, 1991, p. C1.
7. "The Baby-Boomers' Last Whine," *Fortune*, Jan. 27, 1992, p. 56.
8. W. R. Mahler & W. Wrightnour, *Executive Continuity* (Homewood, Ill.: Dow Jones Irwin, 1973).
9. The Myers-Briggs Type Indicator (Consulting Psychologists Press, 1980).
10. M. H. McCormack, *What They Don't Teach at the Harvard Business School* (New York: Bantam, 1986), p. 47.
11. G. B. Graen, *Underwritten Rules for Your Career: 15 Secrets for Fast Track Success* (New York: John Wiley & Sons, 1989), p. 16.
12. Walter R. Trosin, personal interview.
13. C. S. Granrose and J. D. Portwood, "Matching Individual Career Plans and Organizational Career Management," *Academy of Management Journal*, 1987, Vol. 30, No. 4, p. 701.
14. *The Wall Street Journal*, Jan. 9, 1992, p. B1.

Chapter 11: Developing Managers On and Off the Job

1. Roy Yamahiro, personal interview.
2. J. Gordon, "Industry Report 1991—An Overview of Employee Training in America," *Training Magazine*, , Oct. '91, Vol. 28 No 10, p. 31–45.
3. "Back to School—Special Report on Executive Education" *Business Week*, Oct. 28, 1991, p. 102–14.
4. Ibid.
5. M. W. McCall, Jr., M. M. Lombardo, and A. M. Morrison, *The Lessons of Experience: How Successful Executives Develop on the Job* (Lexington, Mass.: Lexington Books, 1988), p. 2.
6. Ibid.
7. Alex Taylor III, "Why Toyota Keeps Getting Better and Better," *Fortune*, Nov. 19, 1990, p. 67.
8. *"Growing a Business Vol. 13*, Paul Hawken on Quad Graphics," Part I 1990, Ambrose Video Publishing Inc., New York. Produced by KQED TV, San Francisco.

9. *Tom Peters: The Leadership Alliance*, produced by Video Publishing House, © 1988 Excell 1, A California Partnership.
10. M. W. McCall, Jr., "Developing Executives Through Work Experiences," *Journal of the Human Resource Planning Society*, Vol. 11, no. 1 (1988), p. 1.
11. *The Lessons of Experience*, p. 6.
12. Ibid., p. 6.
13. Ibid., p. 5.
14. Ibid.
15. Ibid., p. 2.
16. Richard L. Holmberg, personal interview.

Chapter 12: Determining Needs and Readiness.

1. J. M. Bardwick, *The Plateauing Trap* (New York: Bantam Books, 1988), p. 67.
2. V. H. Trimble, *Sam Walton* (New York: Penguin Books, 1990), p. 290.
3. *Houston Chronicle*, Nov. 18, 1990, p. 4E.
4. "Ford Has a Better Management Idea," *Management Review*, January 1992, p. 27.

Chapter 13: Putting It All Together

1. Roy Yamahiro, personal interview.

Index